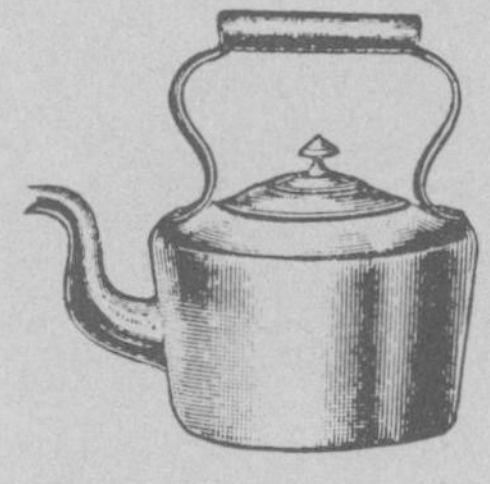

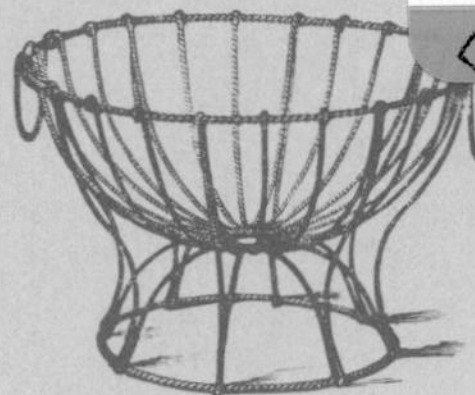

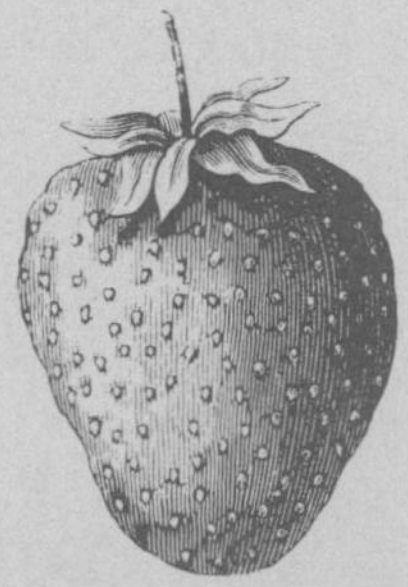

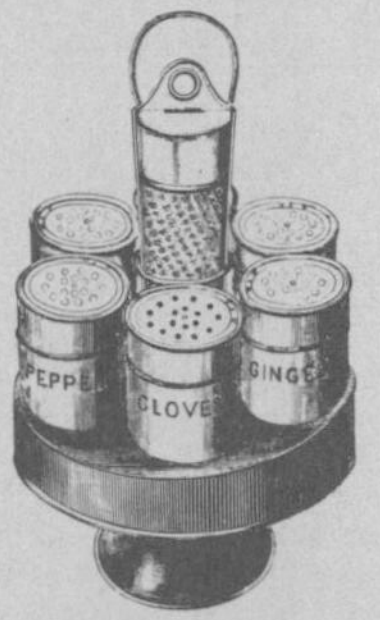

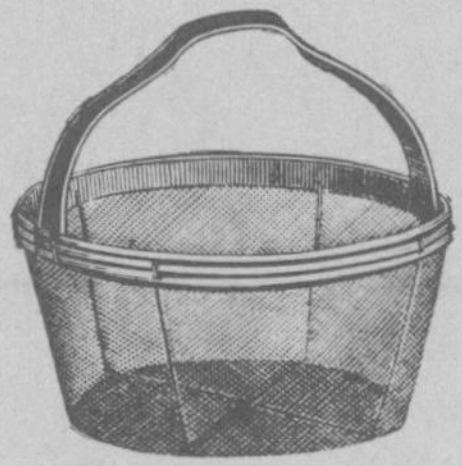

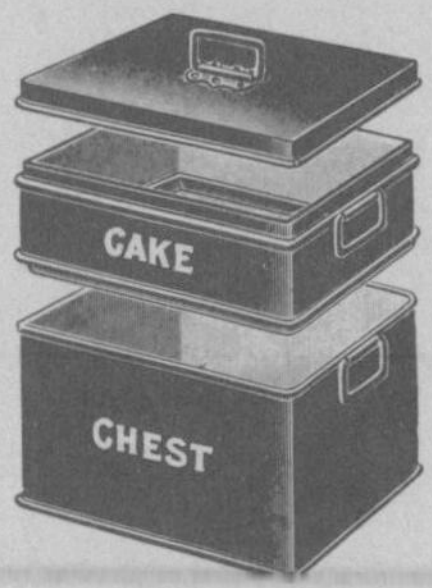
CAKE
CHEST

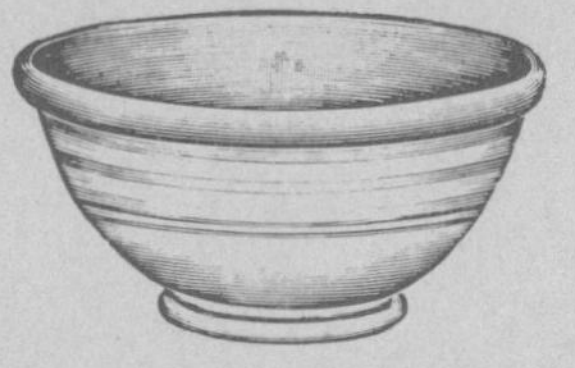

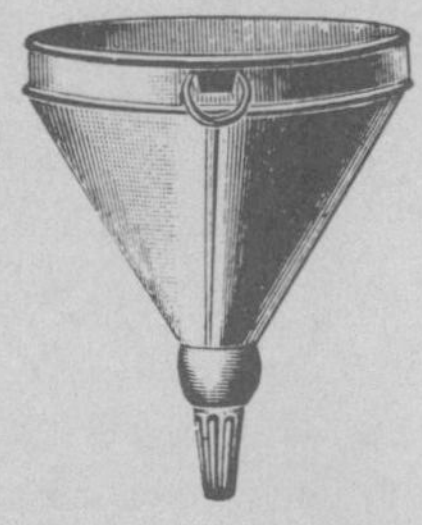

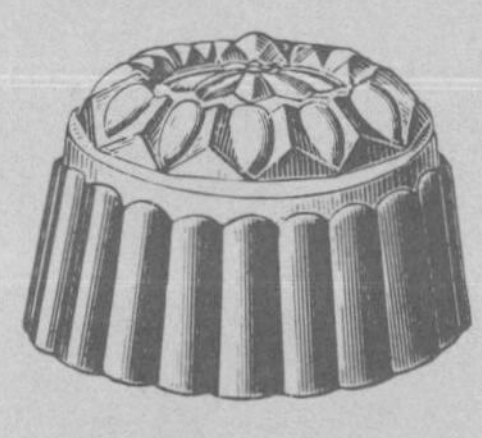

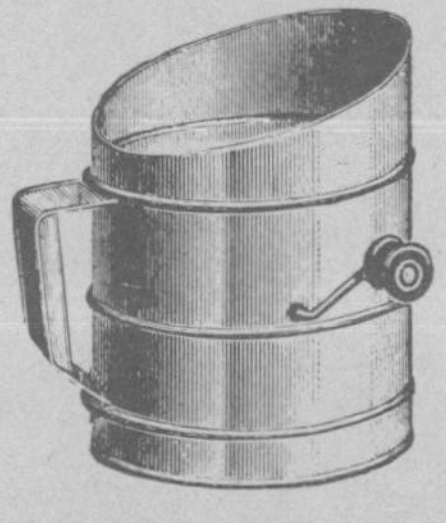

Southern Living

# The SOUTHERN HERITAGE COOKBOOK LIBRARY

# The SOUTHERN HERITAGE
# Soups
## and
# Stews
## COOKBOOK

### OXMOOR HOUSE
Birmingham, Alabama

**Southern Living** ®

**The Southern Heritage Cookbook Library**

Library of Congress Catalog Number: 84-062648
ISBN: 0-8487-0614-5

Manufactured in the United States of America

**The Southern Heritage SOUPS AND STEWS Cookbook**

*Executive Editor:* Ann H. Harvey
*Southern Living*® *Foods Editor:* Jean W. Liles
*Production Editor:* Joan E. Denman
*Foods Editor:* Katherine M. Eakin
*Assistant Foods Editor:* Helen R. Turk
*Director, Test Kitchen:* Laura N. Massey
*Test Kitchen Home Economists:* Kay E. Clarke, Rebecca J. Riddle,
  Elizabeth J. Taliaferro, Dee Waller, Elise Wright Walker
*Production Manager:* Jerry R. Higdon
*Copy Editor:* Melinda E. West
*Editorial Assistants:* Mary Ann Laurens, Karen P. Traccarella
*Food Photographer:* Jim Bathie
*Food Stylist:* Sara Jane Ball
*Layout Designer:* Christian von Rosenvinge
*Mechanical Artist:* Faith Nance
*Research Editors:* Alicia Hathaway, Philip Napoli

**Special Consultants**

*Art Director:* Irwin Glusker
*Heritage Consultant:* Meryle Evans
*Foods Writer:* Lillian B. Marshall
*Food and Recipe Consultants:* Marilyn Wyrick Ingram,
  Audrey P. Stehle

*Cover:* A choice selection of soups and stews includes the ever popular
Vegetable Soup (page 105), Beer Cheese Soup (page 47) topped with
Croutons (page 18), and Prize-Winning Spicy Chili (page 113)
garnished with chopped onions and zucchini. Parmesan Breadsticks
(page 23) and homemade whole wheat bread are favorite
accompaniments. Photograph by Jim Bathie.

# CONTENTS

# INTRODUCTION

No element in Southern menus has been more basic or consistently in favor than the soup and stew family. Colonial cooks, working from tribal memories of childhoods in England, kept the iron stewpot over the fire. In it simmered, by turns, succotash of Indian corn and butterbeans, meats wild or tame, or seafood. With vegetables added in season, meat stews evolved into Brunswick stew or burgoo, meat and seafood went into gumbos or jambalayas, the latter from *jambon*, the French word for ham.

In our early days as a colony, places were set with spoon and knife. Because the morality of the fork, that invention of the Italians (or the Devil) was still being debated in religious England, spoon foods were most practical. Small wonder we find so rich a trove of the delicious "wet foods" in our ancestral attic.

Soup and stew recipes as such, however, were sketchy, mostly personal and transient. The cook placed her faith in the fish and game-getting skills of her husband. She started the kettle and waited to see what the soup du jour would turn out to be. With luck, on that day she created soup.

To a large extent, cooking was picked up by observation and participation, much as good conversation is learned. Southern cooks understood the following principle, as stated in *The Consolidated Library of Modern Cooking*, 1905: " . . . long-continued moist, gentle heat has the effect of rendering tender and grateful the coarser kind of meat that by any other treatment would be unpalatable. . . ." Then, as now, the flesh and bones of mature animals were preferred for stocks: browned first for brown stock, not browned for white.

If the cook added vegetables or dumplings to her soup, she called the mix a stew. Most of those early dishes are still around in some form. Some, like the specialty served at Baltimore's Barnum's Hotel, built in the early 1800s, are rare and scarce. In an excess of niceness, the Barnum's management saw to it that their diamond-back terrapins were exercised in the brick courtyard before hitting the soup pot.

Herewith, then, an update on the good spoonables, from basic savory liquids to the heartiest meal-in-a-bowl.

# THE STOCKPOT

G iven a certified emergency, even the most con-
scientious cook may be forgiven for faking a stock
by dissolving a bouillon cube in hot water. But we
don't want to lose sight of the fact that real stock is
something more; more even than the liquid in which something has been cooked, which is, after all, mere broth. Real
stock has to be *made*. And here we must lament the passing
of the "back of the stove," where the stockpot reposed
throughout a morning or a day. Bones and meat, ripe vegetables, and some herbs sat there, barely simmering, until the
solids had given up their essence into the liquid.

The method has not really changed. To the uninitiated,
it may seem a waste to throw away those solids, but the fact
is they are worthless; the value is all in the stock. No French
chef worthy of the *toque blanche* believes otherwise. Cold
water, barely enough to cover the meat and bones, is used
and brought slowly to boiling. A scum rises and must be
skimmed away as the mixture barely simmers over low heat.
Stock must never actively boil; this causes the scum to mix
with the broth and may cloud it beyond our ability to clarify
it. This is top priority if we intend to use the stock for clear
soups or for aspic.

Stock, after straining and clarification (if indicated), is
poured into clean containers and refrigerated to allow the fat
to rise and solidify. The fat acts as a sealant, so stock will
keep several days if refrigerated. All fat is removed before
using or freezing. Rich stock may be frozen in ice cube trays,
and then placed in freezer bags for longer storage.

Our finished dishes will reflect the difference between
homemade stock and the ubiquitous bouillon cube. Progress
in the commercial food field has seen the rise of true stock
concentrates, containing the real essence of meat or seafood.

A well-flavored, crystal-clear soup gladdens the eye and,
garnished with a julienne of blanched vegetables or strips of
Royal Custard (this presentation was once called Omelet
Soup), makes a memorable first course. Here's how for the
basic stocks, then, as well as suggestions for some distin-
guished accompaniments.

*The way a dish is
presented has much to
do with the manner
in which it is received.
Here, a soup plate of
clear broth is garnished
with baked Soup Nuts.
Deep-fried Parmesan
Rosettes are a crisp,
flavorful accompaniment.*

# BASIC STOCKS

## TO CLARIFY STOCKS OR SOUPS

1 quart clear, liquid-based stock or soup, strained, cooled, degreased, and divided
1 egg white
1 egg shell, crushed

Combine ½ cup stock or soup, egg white, and crushed shell in a small mixing bowl; beat well to combine. Place remaining stock or soup in a Dutch oven; add egg shell mixture, stirring well.

Bring to a boil; boil 3 minutes or until a scum forms on surface of soup. Remove from heat; set aside until scum starts to settle. Strain through several layers of damp cheesecloth. Yield: about 3⅔ cups.

*Note*: Larger quantities of stock or soup may be clarified by increasing egg white and shell proportionately.

## BEEF STOCK

3 pounds beef neck bones
3 quarts water

Place neck bones and water in a stockpot; bring to a boil. Partially cover; reduce heat and simmer 4 hours. Remove from heat, and set aside to cool.

Remove neck bones from stock; set stock aside. Remove meat from bones; discard bones. Reserve meat for other uses. Line a sieve with several layers of damp cheesecloth. Strain stock through sieve into a bowl. Cover and refrigerate stock.

Carefully lift off and discard solidified fat from top of stock. For a clearer stock, see procedure for clarifying stock (left). Use Beef Stock as a foundation for soups and stews. Yield: about 3 cups.

## BROWN ROUX

½ cup vegetable oil
½ cup all-purpose flour

Combine vegetable oil and flour in a 10-inch cast-iron skillet, stirring well to form a smooth paste; cook over low heat, stirring constantly, 50 minutes or until roux is the color of a copper penny. Use Brown Roux as a foundation for gumbos, bisques, or stews. Yield: about ½ cup.

*Note*: Slow cooking over low heat and constant stirring during cooking time are essential in the preparation of a roux to insure a quality product.

*The Excelsior Stove Works promotes its "Hot Blast" model on this trade card, c.1890. Stockpot simmers for all to admire.*

## BROWN STOCK

4½ to 5 pounds beef shin
  bones
2 quarts water
2 medium carrots, sliced
2 stalks celery, sliced
1 medium onion, coarsely
  chopped
1 medium potato, cubed
2 medium turnips, cubed
2 sprigs fresh parsley
10 whole peppercorns
5 whole cloves
1 bay leaf
1 tablespoon salt

Place shin bones in a shallow roasting pan. Bake at 450° for 20 minutes or until well browned, turning occasionally to brown all sides.

Combine browned bones and water in a large stockpot. Let stand 20 minutes. Bring to a boil. Skim surface frequently with a flat ladle to remove grayish scum. Reduce heat; cover and simmer 2 hours. Add remaining ingredients; cover and simmer an additional 2 hours. Remove mixture from heat, and set aside to cool.

Strain stock into a bowl; discard bones, vegetables, and whole spices. Cover and refrigerate stock. Carefully lift off and discard solidified fat from top of stock. For a clearer stock, see procedure for clarifying (page 10). Use Brown Stock as a foundation for soups and stews. Yield: about 1 quart.

## SEASONED SOUP STOCK

2½ pounds beef shank
  bones
2 medium carrots, sliced
1 small onion, peeled and
  quartered
1 stalk celery, halved
1 leek, sliced
1 medium bunch fresh
  parsley
1 teaspoon salt
2 quarts water

Combine all ingredients in a large stockpot. Bring to a boil. Reduce heat; cover and simmer 3 hours.

Strain stock into a bowl; discard bones and vegetables. Cover and refrigerate stock. Carefully lift off and discard solidified fat from top of stock. For a clearer stock, see procedure for clarifying (page 10). Use Seasoned Soup Stock as a foundation for soups and stews. Yield: about 3½ pints.

## WHITE STOCK

2½ pounds meaty veal
  knuckles
½ pound lean veal, cut into
  small cubes
5 cups water
½ small onion
1 stalk celery, cut into pieces
1 small bay leaf
5 whole peppercorns
1½ teaspoons salt

Combine all ingredients in a large stockpot. Place over medium heat, and bring to a boil. Reduce heat to low; cover and simmer 5 hours. Skim surface frequently with a flat ladle to remove grayish scum. Remove from heat, and set aside to cool.

Strain stock into a bowl; discard meat, vegetables, and whole spices. Cover and refrigerate stock. Carefully lift off and discard solidified fat from top of stock. Strain stock through several layers of damp cheesecloth to remove any excess sediment, if desired. Use White Stock as a foundation for other soups and stews. Yield: about 3 cups.

## CHICKEN STOCK

1 (5- to 6-pound) stewing hen
2 quarts water
1 medium onion, quartered
1 stalk celery
1½ teaspoons salt
½ teaspoon pepper

Remove neck and giblets from hen; place in a large stockpot. Rinse hen with cold water, and place in stockpot. Add remaining ingredients. Bring to a boil. Reduce heat; cover and simmer 2 hours, turning hen once after 1 hour. Remove from heat, and set aside to cool.

Strain stock into a bowl; discard neck and giblets. Cover and refrigerate stock. Reserve hen and vegetables for other uses. Carefully lift off and discard solidified fat from top of stock. For a clearer stock, see procedure for clarifying (page 10). Use Chicken Stock as a foundation for soups and stews. Yield: 2 quarts.

# FISH STOCK

2 pounds fish bones and heads
5 cups water
1 small carrot, sliced
1 small onion, sliced
1 stalk celery, cut into pieces
1 sprig fresh parsley
½ bay leaf
Salt and pepper to taste

Combine all ingredients in a large stockpot. Cover and simmer 30 minutes. Strain stock into a bowl; discard bones and vegetables. Cover and refrigerate stock. Carefully lift off and discard solidified fat from top of stock. For a clearer stock, see procedure for clarifying (page 10). Use Fish Stock as a foundation for fish soups and stews. Yield: about 1 quart.

# SEAFOOD STOCK

3 pounds medium shrimp with heads
2 dozen steamed blue crabs
5 quarts water
1 large carrot, sliced
1 large onion, quartered
1 cup coarsely chopped celery
2 teaspoons salt

Remove shrimp heads and shells, reserving both. Set peeled shrimp aside in refrigerator for use in another recipe. Hold 1 steamed crab with both hands, and insert a thumb under the shell by the apron hinge; remove top shell, and set aside. Repeat procedure with remaining crabs. Set aside crabmeat in refrigerator for use in another recipe.

Combine shrimp heads and shells, crab top shells, water, carrot, onion, celery, and salt in a large stockpot. Bring to a boil. Reduce heat; cover and simmer 2 hours. Remove from heat, and cool slightly. Strain stock through several layers of damp cheesecloth, discarding solids. Use Seafood Stock as a foundation for gumbos and stews. Yield: 1 gallon.

# VEGETABLE SOUP MIX

1 gallon peeled, cored, and coarsely chopped tomatoes
2 quarts fresh corn kernels (about 16 ears fresh corn)
1 tablespoon salt
1 tablespoon sugar
1 quart cleaned and sliced okra (about 2 pounds)

Combine all ingredients in a large Dutch oven; bring to a boil. Cook 5 minutes, stirring constantly.

Pour hot mixture into hot pint canning jars, leaving 1-inch headspace. Cover at once with metal lids, and screw bands tight. Process at 10 pounds pressure for 55 minutes. Use Vegetable Soup Mix as a base for soups and stews. Yield: 14 pints.

*Make Vegetable Soup Mix in summer for hearty soup in winter.*

# ADDITIONS TO SOUPS

## HOMEMADE NOODLES

2 cups all-purpose flour
3 eggs
1 tablespoon water
½ teaspoon salt

Place flour on a large wooden board; make a well in center of flour. Break 1 egg into well; draw part of flour into egg, using fingertips of one hand. Add remaining eggs, water, and salt to well; work mixture together with one hand, mixing well. Knead 5 minutes or until smooth and elastic.

Roll dough to 1/16-inch thickness on a lightly floured surface, stretching dough with each roll. Let dough stand 30 minutes or until dry to touch. Roll dough into a scroll, and cut into ¼-inch slices. Unroll noodles, and hang up until completely dry.

Store noodles in airtight containers until ready to use.

Cook noodles in simmering broth or boiling salted water 10 minutes or until tender. Yield: about 6 cups cooked noodles.

## DANISH DUMPLINGS

½ cup milk
¼ cup butter
½ cup all-purpose flour
2 eggs

Combine milk and butter in a medium saucepan; bring to a boil. Add flour all at once, stirring vigorously; cook over medium heat, stirring constantly, until mixture leaves sides of pan and forms a smooth ball. Remove from heat, and cool slightly.

Add eggs, one at a time, beating well after each addition; beat until batter is smooth. Drop batter by teaspoonfuls into simmering soup or stew. Reduce heat; cook, uncovered, 10 minutes. Yield: 4 dozen.

Library of Congress

*Mrs. Alonzo Rushing, a Texan, making dumplings, 1943.*

## ROLLED DUMPLINGS

1½ cups all-purpose flour
2 teaspoons baking powder
¼ teaspoon salt
3 tablespoons butter or margarine
¼ cup plus 2 tablespoons milk

Sift together flour, baking powder, and salt into a medium mixing bowl. Cut in butter using a pastry blender until mixture resembles coarse meal.

Add milk, and stir until dry ingredients are moistened.

Turn dough out onto a lightly floured surface; roll to ¼-inch thickness, and cut with a 1-inch biscuit cutter.

Drop dumplings into simmering soup or stew, allowing room for dumplings to expand during cooking. Reduce heat; cover and simmer 15 minutes or until dumplings are plump and tender. (Do not lift cover during cooking time.) Yield: 4 dozen.

## QUENELLES

½ cup milk
½ cup soft breadcrumbs
1 egg
Dash of salt
Dash of ground nutmeg
Dash of red pepper
⅔ cup uncooked, finely
  chopped chicken breast
1 to 1½ quarts hot chicken
  broth, divided

Combine milk, breadcrumbs, and egg in a medium saucepan; stir until well blended. Cook over low heat, stirring frequently, until mixture thickens. Remove from heat, and stir in salt, nutmeg, and pepper. Cool slightly.

Combine cooled sauce and chicken in container of an electric blender; process until smooth.

Spoon mixture into a pastry bag fitted with a ¼-inch plain tip. Pipe about 1 tablespoon chicken mixture into a small "S" shape in a large buttered skillet. Repeat procedure with remaining mixture, spacing quenelles 1 inch apart, until surface of skillet is covered.

Pour hot chicken broth very slowly down the sides of skillet so as not to disturb quenelles, adding enough broth to cover quenelles. Cover and simmer 4 minutes or until quenelles float to surface of broth. Remove cooked quenelles with a slotted spoon; drain on paper towels. Pour off broth, and set aside. Repeat procedure with remaining chicken mixture and reserved broth.

Add quenelles to remaining hot chicken broth or other broths or consommés before serving. Yield: 6 to 8 servings.

*Garnishes for clear soups, clockwise: S-shaped Quenelles, Danish Dumplings (page 13), and Homemade Noodles (page 13).*

## BREAD AND BUTTER BALLS

2 cups soft breadcrumbs
2 tablespoons chopped
  fresh parsley
1 teaspoon grated onion
½ teaspoon baking
  powder
¼ teaspoon salt
Pinch of pepper
2 eggs, beaten
3 tablespoons butter or
  margarine, melted
1 tablespoon milk

Combine breadcrumbs, parsley, onion, baking powder, salt, and pepper in a medium mixing bowl; stir until well combined. Add eggs, butter, and milk, stirring well.

Shape mixture by heaping teaspoonfuls into balls; place on baking sheets or plates. Cover and refrigerate at least 30 minutes or until ready to use.

Add balls to simmering soup or stew, allowing room for balls to expand during cooking. Reduce heat; cover and simmer 10 minutes. (Do not lift cover during cooking time.) Repeat procedure with remaining balls, if necessary. Yield: about 2½ dozen.

## RICE BALLS

⅔ cup cooked regular rice
1 egg
2 tablespoons plus 1½
  teaspoons all-purpose
  flour
1 tablespoon chopped
  fresh parsley
1 teaspoon grated onion
⅛ teaspoon salt
⅛ teaspoon pepper

Place rice in a small mixing bowl; mash. Add egg, flour, parsley, onion, salt, and pepper, mixing well.

Drop dough by teaspoonfuls into simmering broth or consommé, allowing room for balls to expand during cooking. Reduce heat; cover and simmer 5 minutes. (Do not lift cover during cooking time.) Yield: 1 dozen.

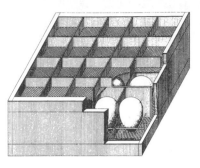

## EGG BALLS

4 hard-cooked egg yolks
¼ teaspoon salt
¼ teaspoon pepper
1 egg white
2 tablespoons all-purpose
  flour
2 tablespoons butter or
  margarine

Press egg yolks through a sieve into a small mixing bowl; add salt, pepper, and egg white, stirring well. Shape mixture into ¾-inch balls; roll in flour.

Melt butter in a small skillet over medium heat. Sauté a few balls at a time until lightly browned. Add to hot broths or consommés just before serving. Yield: about 1½ dozen.

While clear soups are a joy forever, they are even more attractive when we drop in some tasty bites such as the ones on this page. Quenelles are a French dumpling made of forcemeat (smoothly ground chicken, fish, etc.), bound with flour, and gently poached in broth. Small balls made of bread and butter or rice simmer in broth, expanding as they cook; sautéed balls made of yolks of hard-cooked eggs are equally savory embellishments. Any one of these additions elevates a clear broth to "gourmet" status.

*The right and wrong way to carry a bird.*

## SPAETZLE

2 eggs
1½ cups all-purpose flour
½ cup water
½ teaspoon salt
¼ teaspoon baking powder
Dash of white pepper
Dash of nutmeg

Beat eggs in a medium mixing bowl until light and fluffy. Add flour and water alternately, beginning and ending with flour; beat well after each addition. Stir in remaining ingredients, mixing well.

Bring 2 quarts water to a simmering boil in a small Dutch oven. Place a greased spaetzle colander or regular colander over water. Place spaetzle mixture into colander; press mixture through colander into water. Cook, uncovered, 5 minutes, stirring frequently. Drain.

Spoon spaetzle into hot broths or consommés just before serving. Yield: 4 cups.

## ROYAL CUSTARD

3 egg yolks
1 egg
1 cup chicken broth

Combine yolks and egg in a small mixing bowl; beat well. Gradually add chicken broth, beating until well blended. Pour mixture into a well-greased 10- x 6- x 2-inch baking dish. Place baking dish in a 13- x 9- x 2-inch baking pan. Pour hot water into pan to a depth of 1 inch.

Bake, uncovered, at 350° for 25 minutes or until a knife inserted halfway between center and edge of custard comes out clean. Remove baking dish from pan. Cool custard to room temperature in baking dish. Cut custard into various shapes with miniature aspic cutters. Remove from dish.

Use Royal Custard as a garnish for hot broths or consommés. Yield: 8 servings.

## MATZO BALLS

2 green onions, chopped
2 tablespoons butter or margarine
¾ cup matzo meal
1 cup boiling water
2 eggs, beaten
¼ cup chopped almonds
¼ cup chopped fresh parsley
½ teaspoon salt
About 5 cups chicken broth

Sauté onion in butter in a small skillet over medium heat until tender. Combine sautéed onion, meal, and water in a small mixing bowl, stirring until water is absorbed. Set aside to cool.

Add eggs, almonds, chopped parsley, and salt to cooled mixture, mixing well. Cover and refrigerate until thoroughly chilled. Shape mixture into twenty-four 1-inch balls.

Bring chicken broth to a boil; add matzo balls to broth, allowing room for balls to expand during cooking. Reduce heat; cover and simmer 15 minutes. (Do not lift cover during cooking time.) Yield: 2 dozen.

# ACCOMPANIMENTS

## JULIENNE GARNISH

2 medium carrots, scraped
  and cut into 2- x ⅛-inch
  strips
2 medium turnips, peeled and
  cut into 2- x ⅛-inch strips
1 gallon boiling water

Combine all ingredients in a large Dutch oven. Bring to a boil. Reduce heat; simmer, uncovered, 10 minutes. Drain. Use julienne strips as a garnish for hot broths or consommés. Yield: 2⅔ cups.

*Note*: Squash and zucchini strips may be substituted for carrot and turnip strips; reduce cooking time to 2 minutes.

*A horse-drawn "truck"
is delivering an amazing
variety of cereals on this
1890 trade card for
AMC Perfect Cereals.*

## FRENCH-FRIED PEANUTS

1 pound raw peanuts, shelled
Vegetable oil
Salt to taste
Cream or thick soup

Place shelled peanuts in a single layer in a 15- x 10- x 1-inch jellyroll pan. Bake at 350° for 15 minutes. Remove from oven, and cool. Remove hulls from peanuts.

Fry peanuts in a wire basket in deep, hot oil (300°) until lightly browned. (Peanuts will continue to brown after removed from oil.) Drain well on unglazed brown paper. (Do not use recycled paper.) Sprinkle peanuts with salt. Coarsely chop peanuts, and use as a garnish for cream soups. Yield: about 1½ cups.

## CEREAL BITS

2 cups bite-size shredded
  wheat cereal

Place cereal on a baking sheet in a single layer. Broil 6 inches from heating element until cereal is lightly toasted, stirring as necessary. Use Cereal Bits as a garnish for soups or stews. Yield: 2 cups.

*Note*: Toasted oat cereal may be substituted for shredded wheat cereal.

*Saleslady prepares an order in the cake, cracker, and bread section of a Washington, D.C. area market, c.1915.*

## SOUP NUTS

2 cups all-purpose flour
1 teaspoon salt
3 eggs, lightly beaten
2 tablespoons vegetable oil

Combine flour and salt in a medium mixing bowl; mix well. Stir in eggs and oil until dry ingredients are moistened. Turn dough out onto a lightly floured surface; knead lightly 3 to 4 times.

Divide dough into 5 equal portions. Shape each portion into a 12-inch rope. Cut each rope into ¼-inch segments. Place segments on ungreased baking sheets. Bake at 375° for 12 minutes or until lightly browned, shaking pan occasionally. Serve Soup Nuts with hot soups or stews. Yield: about 4 cups.

## CROUTONS

6 slices bread
Vegetable oil

Remove crust from bread slices. Cut bread into ⅜-inch cubes. Drop cubes into deep, hot oil (375°), and cook until lightly browned. Remove with a slotted spoon; drain. Serve Croutons with soups or stews. Yield: about 3½ cups.

### Baked Croutons:

Place bread cubes on an ungreased baking sheet. Bake at 350°, stirring occasionally, for 20 minutes or until crisp and lightly browned.

### Cheese Croutons:

Place 1 cup Croutons (either deep-fried or baked) in a greased 15- x 10- x 1-inch jellyroll pan. Sprinkle ½ cup (2 ounces) shredded Cheddar cheese and ¼ teaspoon garlic powder over croutons. Bake at 350° for 3 minutes or until cheese melts.

## SIPPETS

6 slices bread
Melted butter or margarine

Remove crust from bread. Cut each slice into 4 triangles; brush both sides with butter. Place on a baking sheet. Broil 6 inches from heating element 2 minutes on each side or until lightly toasted. Serve with soups or stews. Yield: 2 dozen.

## CORNMEAL SIPPETS

1 cup cornmeal
1¼ cups boiling water
2 tablespoons shortening, melted
½ teaspoon salt

Combine all ingredients in a small mixing bowl; mix well. Spoon batter by tablespoonfuls onto a lightly greased baking sheet. Bake at 400° for 15 minutes or until edges are browned. Serve warm with soups or stews. Yield: 1½ dozen.

## QUICK-FRIED CHEESE ROLLS

24 slices fresh white bread, crust removed
½ pound sharp Cheddar cheese, cut into ½- x ½- x 2-inch pieces
Vegetable oil

Using a rolling pin, flatten each bread slice. Place a strip of cheese on each slice. Roll up slices jellyroll fashion; wrap each roll in waxed paper. Place seam side down on a baking sheet; refrigerate 30 minutes.

Remove rolls from waxed paper; deep fry in hot oil (375°) until golden brown. Drain well. Serve warm with soups or stews. Yield: 2 dozen.

## CHEESE FINGERS

1 cup all-purpose flour
¼ teaspoon salt
¼ cup plus 2 tablespoons shortening
2 to 3 tablespoons cold water
¼ cup grated Parmesan cheese
Dash of salt
Dash of pepper
Sifted powdered sugar

Combine flour and ¼ teaspoon salt in a small bowl; cut in shortening with a pastry blender until mixture resembles coarse meal. Sprinkle water over surface of mixture; stir with a fork until dry ingredients are moistened. Shape dough into a ball; cover and chill.

Roll dough to ⅛-inch thickness on a floured surface; trim to a 12- x 10-inch rectangle. Cut pastry into twelve 5- x 2-inch rectangles. Combine cheese, dash of salt, and pepper. Sprinkle 1 teaspoon cheese mixture over surface of each portion, leaving a ¼-inch margin on all sides. Moisten edges with water; fold over to form a rectangle. Press edges together to seal.

Place on an ungreased baking sheet. Bake at 450° for 12 minutes or until lightly browned. Cool slightly; sprinkle with powdered sugar. Serve warm with soups or stews. Yield: 1 dozen.

## CHEESE TOAST

8 slices bread
1 cup (4 ounces) shredded sharp Cheddar cheese, softened
2 tablespoons whipping cream
2 teaspoons prepared mustard
¼ teaspoon Worcestershire sauce
Sweet pickles

Remove crust from bread; toast bread until lightly browned on both sides, and set aside.

Combine cheese, whipping cream, mustard, and Worcestershire sauce in a small bowl, mixing until well blended. Spread reserved toast with cheese mixture. Place toast on a 15- x 10- x 1-inch jellyroll pan; broil 4 to 5 inches from heating element just until cheese melts. Serve immediately with pickles as an accompaniment to soups or stews. Yield: 8 servings.

Collection of Kit Barry, Brattleboro, Vermont

*Heinz already had 57 varieties back in 1890, according to reverse side of this trade card.*

*1854 engraving shows women making butter.*

Library of Congress

# SOUFFLÉED CRACKERS

24 saltine crackers
2 tablespoons butter or margarine, melted
⅛ teaspoon salt

Soak crackers in ice water in a large bowl for 3 minutes or until soft. Remove crackers with a slotted spoon, and drain 5 minutes. Carefully place crackers on baking sheets; brush with melted butter, and sprinkle with salt. Bake at 450° for 15 minutes or until crisp and golden brown. Serve immediately with soups or stews. Yield: 2 dozen.

# GARNISH FOR CREAM SOUPS

1 (3-ounce) package cream cheese, softened
40 round buttery crackers
Paprika
1 teaspoon finely chopped fresh parsley

Beat cream cheese in a small mixing bowl with an electric mixer until light and fluffy; spoon into a pastry bag fitted with a ¼-inch star tip. Pipe a small amount of cream cheese onto each cracker. Sprinkle each lightly with paprika and parsley. Serve crackers with cream soups. Yield: 40 crackers.

# CHEESEBITS

24 saltine crackers
¼ pound sharp Cheddar cheese, cut into ¼-inch-thick slices

Place crackers on an ungreased baking sheet; top each cracker with a cheese slice. Broil 6 inches from heating element 2 minutes or until cheese melts. Serve immediately with soups or stews. Yield: 2 dozen.

# SESAME CRISPS

1¾ cups all-purpose flour
½ cup cornmeal
2 tablespoons sugar
½ teaspoon baking soda
¼ teaspoon salt
¼ cup butter or margarine, softened
½ cup water
2 tablespoons vinegar
¼ cup butter or margarine, melted
½ cup sesame seeds

Combine flour, cornmeal, sugar, soda, and salt in a large mixing bowl; mix well. Cut in softened butter with a pastry blender until mixture resembles coarse meal. Combine water and vinegar; add to flour mixture, stirring until dry ingredients are moistened.

Turn dough out onto a floured surface; knead 4 to 5 times. (Dough will be soft.)

Shape dough into ½-inch balls. Using a floured rolling pin, roll each ball into a 2-inch circle. Transfer circles to ungreased baking sheets. Brush each with melted butter; sprinkle with sesame seeds. Using a spatula, press sesame seeds firmly into crackers. Bake at 375° for 10 minutes or until lightly browned. Remove crackers from baking sheets, and cool on wire racks. Serve with soups or stews. Yield: about 2 dozen.

# SODA CRACKERS

4 cups all-purpose flour
1 teaspoon baking soda
½ teaspoon salt
1 tablespoon butter or margarine
1 tablespoon lard or shortening
1 egg, beaten
2 cups buttermilk

Combine flour, soda, and salt in a large mixing bowl; cut in butter, lard, and egg with a pastry blender until mixture resembles coarse meal. Add buttermilk, stirring well.

Turn dough out onto a floured surface. Pound dough with a wooden mallet or rolling pin for 20 minutes or until surface is covered with air bubbles, folding dough over frequently.

Roll dough to ⅛-inch thickness, and cut into 2-inch squares. Place on well-greased baking sheets in even rows, and prick tops of squares with tines of a fork. Bake at 400° for 15 minutes or until lightly browned. Remove crackers from baking sheets, and serve with soups or stews. Yield: about 6 dozen.

*Making Soda Crackers (front) is a little like making beaten biscuits. Souffléed Crackers are a breeze.*

## PARMESAN BREADSTICKS

1 package dry yeast
1 tablespoon honey
1½ cups lukewarm water
   (105° to 115°)
3½ to 4½ cups all-purpose
   flour, divided
1½ cups grated Parmesan
   cheese
Melted butter
Coarse salt

Dissolve yeast and honey in lukewarm water in a large mixing bowl; let stand 5 minutes. Gradually add 3 cups flour and cheese, beating at low speed of an electric mixer until smooth. Gradually add enough remaining flour to make a soft dough.

Turn dough out onto a lightly floured surface; knead 6 to 8 minutes or until smooth and elastic.

Divide dough into fourths. Clip each fourth into 12 equal portions, using a pair of kitchen shears. Roll each portion into a pencil-like stick 8 inches long. Place sticks about 1 inch apart on greased baking sheets. Brush with melted butter; sprinkle with coarse salt. Cover and let rise in a warm place (85°), free from drafts, 30 minutes or until doubled in bulk.

Bake at 400° for 10 to 15 minutes or until golden brown. Serve with soups or stews. Yield: 4 dozen.

*Pillsbury Flour trade card, c.1890. The Pillsbury family has been active in the operation of the company for several generations.*

## PARMESAN ROSETTES

3 eggs, beaten
1½ cups milk
1¼ cups all-purpose flour
¼ cup wheat germ
2 tablespoons minced dried
   onion
2 tablespoons grated
   Parmesan cheese
1 tablespoon sugar
Vegetable oil
Additional grated Parmesan
   cheese

Combine eggs and milk in a medium mixing bowl; beat well. Combine flour, wheat germ, onion, 2 tablespoons cheese, and sugar in a small mixing bowl; add to egg mixture, beating until well blended.

Heat 2 to 3 inches of oil in a small Dutch oven or large skillet to 375°. Dip rosette iron into hot oil; drain off excess oil. Dip hot iron halfway into batter; return to oil, and cook 1 minute or until golden brown. Remove from hot oil. Gently loosen rosette from iron; drain well on paper towels. Sprinkle with additional cheese, and cool completely on a wire rack. Repeat procedure with remaining batter. Serve with soups or stews. Yield: about 3 dozen.

*Note*: Rosettes may be stored in an airtight container.

Notice the third pinion

## WHEAT CRACKERS

1 cup whole wheat flour
1 cup all-purpose flour
¼ cup plus 1 tablespoon
   sugar
2 teaspoons baking powder
1 teaspoon baking soda
½ teaspoon cream of tartar
½ teaspoon salt
½ cup butter or margarine
¾ cup buttermilk

Combine dry ingredients in a medium mixing bowl. Cut in butter with a pastry blender until mixture resembles coarse meal. Add buttermilk; stir with a fork until dry ingredients are moistened.

Turn dough out onto a lightly floured surface; roll to ⅛-inch thickness. Cut into assorted shapes with cookie cutters; place crackers 1 inch apart on ungreased baking sheets. Prick top of each cracker several times with tines of a fork. Bake at 350° for 15 minutes or until lightly browned. Cool on wire racks. Serve with soups or stews. Yield: about 6 dozen.

*Note*: Crackers may be stored in airtight containers.

## MEXICAN CORNBREAD

1½ cups self-rising cornmeal
2 tablespoons sugar
½ teaspoon salt
1¼ cups milk
¼ cup plus 2 tablespoons
   vegetable oil
2 eggs, beaten
1 (8¾-ounce) can cream-style
   corn
1 large onion, finely chopped
¾ cup (3 ounces) shredded
   sharp Cheddar cheese
1 to 2 jalapeño peppers,
   chopped

Combine dry ingredients in a large mixing bowl; add milk, oil, and eggs, mixing well. Stir in remaining ingredients. Pour batter into an ungreased 10-inch cast-iron skillet. Bake at 400° for 40 minutes. Cool slightly, and cut into wedges to serve. Yield: 8 to 10 servings.

# THE LIGHTER SIDE

Moving from broth to bouillon is merely a matter of substituting a French word for an English one. Hannah Glasse counseled that good broth is simmered " . . . softly, don't put too much more water than you intend to have soop [sic] or broth . . . cover it close, and set it on embers. . . . " Such delicious hot liquids traditionally were served with sippets or toasted penny loaves or saved to use in sauces, gravies, or "made dishes." To make the original "bouillon cube," innovative cooks simmered finished broth without a lid until it was reduced to a third of its volume. Poured into a shallow dish, it jelled firmly enough to be cut and stored dry. This "portable soup" was convenient for home use or for travelers, who had only to add water for a nourishing soup.

Consommé is beef broth (veal bones add gelatine content) made of the same ingredients as bouillon, but the meat is cooked in previously prepared broth instead of water to intensify the flavor. Perfectly made consommé is treated with egg whites and egg shells to precipitate the dregs left after straining. The result is limpidly clear and delicious hot or cold. Chilled consommé Madrilene, softly gelatinous and delicately tinged with pink, is a summertime first course without peer. For clear soup, Hannah Glasse again: "First take great care the pots or saucepans and covers be very clean and free from all grease and sand. . . . " We no longer use sand to clean cookware, of course, but pot-washing has not gone out of fashion!

Fruit soups are Scandinavian in origin. The Swedes traditionally served them either as appetizer or dessert. Oddly, as fruit soups have gained in popularity in this country, they seem to have lost ground in their native land. In Finland, blueberries are dried to be used in a sweet soup which is assumed to be beneficial to the stomach. Translated to our ingredients, fruit soups in the South use fresh peaches, strawberries, papayas — all the good seasonal, regional fruits to make refreshing soups for either end of a meal.

There's a world of goodness to be found in these lighter soups.

*All the soups pictured here have in common a liquid base. For a light first course, serve Jellied Consommé (front) in your nicest china. Robust Huguenot Onion Soup (right) needs oven-going bowls. For dessert, Cold Peach-Orange Soup.*

# BOUILLONS & CONSOMMÉS

## ICED BOUILLON

2 chicken-flavored bouillon
   cubes
2 cups boiling water
3 tablespoons sherry
Chopped fresh chives
   (optional)

Combine bouillon cubes and boiling water, stirring until bouillon dissolves. Cool mixture completely. Stir in sherry; cover and chill thoroughly.

Serve in chilled bowls as an appetizer; garnish with chives, if desired. Yield: 2 cups.

*The ice wagon
"cometh" on Ranson
Street in Chapel Hill,
North Carolina, 1927.*

## BEEF BOUILLON

2 pounds lean beef for
   stewing, cut into 1-inch
   cubes
2 tablespoons vegetable oil
2 quarts water
2 stalks celery, thinly sliced
1 carrot, thinly sliced
1 thick slice onion
1 teaspoon salt
6 whole peppercorns
2 whole cloves
Lemon twists (optional)

Brown meat in oil in a large Dutch oven. Stir in remaining ingredients except lemon twists; mix well, and bring to a boil. Reduce heat; simmer, uncovered, 3 hours. Remove from heat, and cool slightly.

Line a sieve with several layers of damp cheesecloth. Strain mixture through sieve into a bowl. Cover and refrigerate bouillon overnight. Discard whole peppercorns and cloves. Reserve meat and vegetables for use in other recipes.

Skim off and discard any fat that has risen to top of bouillon. Clarify bouillon according to procedure (page 10).

Serve bouillon warm or chilled as an appetizer. Garnish each serving with a lemon twist, if desired. Yield: 2½ cups.

*Note:* Bouillon may be used as a foundation for other soups or stews or in other recipes.

*Tomato Bouillon, with a slice of lemon, makes a light appetizer. Old-South Vegetable Bouillon is basic to many recipes.*

## OLD-SOUTH VEGETABLE BOUILLON

1½ pounds turnip greens, cleaned
1 (28-ounce) can whole tomatoes, undrained
1 (14½-ounce) can whole tomatoes, undrained
Salt and pepper to taste

Place greens in a medium Dutch oven; add tomatoes. Cook over low heat until steam begins to form. Cover and cook 1½ hours, stirring occasionally. Remove from heat, and cool slightly.

Strain cooled mixture through cheesecloth; discard turnip greens and tomato pulp. Clarify bouillon according to procedure (page 10).

Season bouillon with salt and pepper. Serve bouillon warm or chilled as an appetizer or use as a foundation for other soups or stews. Yield: about 3 cups.

## TOMATO BOUILLON

2 (14½-ounce) cans whole tomatoes, undrained
2 cups water
1 thick slice onion
12 whole peppercorns
4 whole cloves
1 bay leaf
2 teaspoons salt
2 teaspoons sugar
Lemon slices (optional)

Combine all ingredients except lemon slices in a large saucepan; bring to a boil. Reduce heat; cover and simmer 20 minutes, stirring occasionally. Strain mixture through cheesecloth; discard vegetables and spices. Serve bouillon warm or chilled as an appetizer. Garnish each serving with a lemon slice, if desired. Yield: 1 quart.

Our appreciation of homemade clear soups appears to have waned with the passing of the wood- or coal-fired stove. Historically, however, scarcely an elegant multi-course dinner of the nineteenth or early twentieth century left off the rich liquid first course. "Bouillon, Petit Toast" was printed at the top of a lengthy menu for an alumni dinner at the University of Virginia in 1892. It was preceded by "Mint Julep, Old Virginia Style." Clear green turtle soup was immensely popular along the East Coast until the green sea turtle approached extinction. The heat under the modern stockpot can be tempered by an asbestos pad over gas flame or a wire trivet on an electric burner.

# BEEF CONSOMMÉ

1 pound soup bones
3 pounds beef stew meat, cut into 1½-inch cubes and divided
3 pounds veal knuckles
3 quarts cold water
1 quart chicken broth
1 small onion, sliced
1 carrot, thinly sliced
1 small turnip, diced
1 stalk celery, thinly sliced
1 teaspoon salt
1 teaspoon whole peppercorns
1 bay leaf
4 whole cloves
1 sprig fresh marjoram
2 sprigs fresh parsley
2 sprigs fresh thyme
Chopped fresh parsley

Remove 2 tablespoons marrow from soup bones; set bones aside. Combine marrow and 1½ pounds stew meat in a large skillet; cook over medium heat until meat is browned.

Combine reserved bones, browned meat mixture, remaining stew meat, veal knuckles, and water in a large stockpot. Let stand 30 minutes. Bring to a boil over medium heat. Reduce heat; cover and simmer 3 hours. Add chicken broth; cover and simmer an additional 2 hours. Remove from heat, and cool slightly. Strain through a colander into a large stockpot, reserving meat for other uses. Discard bones. Cover and refrigerate consommé overnight; skim off and discard congealed fat that has risen to the surface.

Place consommé over medium heat; add onion, carrot, turnip, celery, salt, peppercorns, bay leaf, cloves, marjoram, parsley sprigs, and thyme. Bring to a boil. Reduce heat; cover and simmer 1½ hours. Remove from heat, and cool slightly. Strain through several layers of damp cheesecloth into a Dutch oven, discarding vegetables and spices. Clarify consommé according to procedure (page 10).

Serve consommé warm or chilled as an appetizer. Garnish each serving with chopped parsley. Yield: 3½ quarts.

*Project for a farm family, 1919, was cutting up and preparing beef for preservation.*

National Archives

# VEGETABLE CONSOMMÉ

2 gallons water
2 veal knuckles
1 bunch celery, cut into
 ½-inch slices
4 medium potatoes,
 quartered
2 medium turnips, quartered
1 medium onion, quartered
¼ medium cabbage, coarsely
 chopped
1 carrot, thinly sliced
1 (14½-ounce) can whole
 tomatoes, undrained
1 tablespoon salt
4 whole cloves
1 tablespoon butter or
 margarine
2 tablespoons firmly packed
 brown sugar
2 eggs

Combine water, veal knuckles, celery, potatoes, turnips, onion, cabbage, carrot, tomatoes, salt, and cloves in a large stockpot; bring to a boil. Cover and cook over high heat 6 hours. Remove from heat, and cool to room temperature.

Strain mixture through several layers of damp cheesecloth, discarding veal knuckles, vegetables, and cloves. Cover and refrigerate broth overnight.

Skim off and discard any fat which has risen to the surface. Melt butter in a small saucepan over low heat; add brown sugar and cook, stirring constantly, over low heat until mixture browns. Remove from heat, and set aside.

Separate eggs, reserving yolks for other uses; coarsely crumble egg shells. Combine egg shells and egg whites in a medium mixing bowl; add to consommé, and bring to a boil. Cook over high heat 1 minute. Stir in browned sugar mixture, and continue cooking 1 minute. Remove from heat, and let stand until all sediment settles out. Strain mixture through several layers of damp cheesecloth, discarding egg shells and egg white sediment.

Serve consommé warm or chilled as an appetizer. Yield: about 1½ quarts.

*Colorful page from Peter Henderson's 1899 seed catalogue.*

## JELLIED CONSOMMÉ

2 envelopes unflavored
 gelatin
½ cup cold water
3 cups beef consommé
¼ cup dry sherry
½ teaspoon lemon juice
Fresh parsley sprigs
Lemon slices, halved

Soften gelatin in water. Bring consommé to a boil in a medium saucepan; remove from heat. Add softened gelatin, stirring until well blended. Stir in sherry and lemon juice. Transfer to a large bowl; cool to room temperature. Chill overnight.

Cut jellied consommé with a fork; spoon into appetizer serving bowls. Garnish with parsley sprigs and halved lemon slices. Yield: 6 to 8 appetizer servings.

## WINE CONSOMMÉ

1 (10¾-ounce) can beef
 consommé, undiluted
1½ cups tomato juice
½ cup rosé wine
Commercial sour cream
Chopped fresh chives

Combine consommé and tomato juice in a medium saucepan; simmer over medium heat until thoroughly heated. Stir in wine, and simmer an additional 2 minutes.

Serve consommé warm or chilled as an appetizer soup. Garnish each serving with a dollop of sour cream, and sprinkle with chopped chives. Yield: about 3½ cups.

## MADRILENE

1 parsnip
6 whole cloves
3 bay leaves
1 small bunch fresh parsley
1 veal knuckle
2 pounds boneless round
   steak, cut into 1-inch
   cubes
3 carrots, sliced
1 large turnip, sliced
2 stalks celery, cut into
   1-inch pieces
1 clove garlic, sliced
10 whole peppercorns
1 tablespoon plus ½ teaspoon
   salt, divided
5 quarts water
2 envelopes unflavored
   gelatin
2 tablespoons beet juice
   (optional)
½ teaspoon celery salt
¼ teaspoon pepper
Fresh parsley sprigs

Stud parsnip with cloves; set aside. Tie bay leaves and parsley together with string; set aside.

Combine veal knuckle and round steak in a large stockpot. Add studded parsnip, parsley-bay leaf bunch, carrots, turnip, celery, garlic, peppercorns, 2½ teaspoons salt, and water. Bring slowly to a boil. Reduce heat; simmer, uncovered, 5 hours. Remove scum when necessary. Remove stockpot from heat, and cool slightly.

Strain mixture through a large colander or sieve lined with several layers of damp cheesecloth. (Discard meat and vegetables.) Return broth to clean stockpot; cover and refrigerate overnight.

Carefully lift off and discard solidified fat from top of broth. Clarify broth according to procedure (page 10).

Dissolve gelatin in a small amount of hot broth; add to remaining hot broth, stirring well. Stir in beet juice, if desired, to add color. Stir in remaining salt, celery salt, and pepper. Chill thoroughly.

Serve chilled in individual soup bowls. Garnish each serving with parsley sprigs. Yield: 3 quarts.

*Sour cream and caviar put the "Russe" in Madrilene.*

## MADRILENE À LA RUSSE

1 (13-ounce) can red
   madrilene
1 (8-ounce) carton
   commercial sour cream
Caviar
Fresh parsley or watercress
   sprigs

Place unopened can of madrilene in refrigerator 2 hours or until partially set. (Madrilene should resemble consistency of unbeaten egg white.) Pour madrilene into a medium mixing bowl; add sour cream, beating with a wire whisk until well blended. Cover and refrigerate 4 to 5 hours or until mixture thickens and begins to jell.

Spoon into chilled serving bowls. Garnish with caviar and parsley or watercress. Serve as an appetizer. Yield: 3 cups.

## CLAM MADRILENE

2 (13-ounce) cans beef
   consommé madrilene,
   chilled
1½ cups clam juice
1 tablespoon lemon juice
1 tablespoon chopped fresh
   dill
1 tablespoon chopped chives
1 teaspoon grated lemon rind
⅛ teaspoon dried whole
   tarragon
½ cup commercial sour
   cream
Chopped fresh parsley

Combine first 7 ingredients in a large bowl, stirring well. Cover and chill thoroughly. Fold in sour cream just before serving. Spoon into individual glasses or bowls. Garnish each serving with chopped parsley. Serve chilled as an appetizer or first course. Yield: about 1 quart.

# FAMILY FAVORITES

## FRENCH BROTH

2 pounds beef short ribs
1 pound veal, cut into cubes
1 (5- to 6-pound) hen, cut up
5 quarts water
1 (1-pound) cabbage, quartered
1 pound spinach
1 (1-pound) lettuce, quartered
1 tablespoon salt
¼ teaspoon whole peppercorns
⅛ teaspoon ground mace
½ pound beef skirt steak, cut into ½-inch cubes
2 tablespoons butter or margarine

Combine first 4 ingredients in a 14-quart stockpot. Bring to a boil. Cook 5 minutes; remove scum. Add cabbage, spinach, lettuce, salt, peppercorns, and mace. Bring to a boil. Reduce heat; simmer, uncovered, 4 hours. Remove from heat; cool slightly, and strain broth through cheesecloth. Reserve beef, veal, and hen for other uses. Cover and chill broth thoroughly; skim and discard fat from broth, setting broth aside.

Sauté skirt steak in butter in a medium skillet until browned. Add ½ cup broth; cover and simmer 10 minutes or until tender.

Heat remaining broth thoroughly. Stir in steak mixture. Spoon into individual serving bowls. Serve immediately. Yield: 2 quarts.

Clear liquid soups require special care in garnishing, lest their clarity be mistaken for invisibility. French Broth has little cubes of beef added for interest, while Beef Soup comes with tiny Liver Dumplings to relieve the plainness. But when no solids are included in the soup itself, we can always fall back on chopped parsley or a sprig of watercress on top. When caviar is used, add it at the last minute; the color "bleeds" on standing.

*"An American Farmyard - A Frosty Morning,"* Harper's Weekly, *1877.*

*Artist works as shadow-maker performs on 1895 trade card for Robinson's Barley.*

## BEEF SOUP WITH LIVER DUMPLINGS

1½ pounds round steak, cut into 1-inch cubes
1 (14½-ounce) can whole tomatoes, drained and chopped
1 small onion, quartered
1 carrot, sliced
1 stalk celery, cut into 2-inch pieces
3 whole allspice
1¼ teaspoons salt, divided
½ teaspoon pepper, divided
1½ quarts water
¼ pound beef liver
12 saltine crackers
2 eggs, beaten
¼ cup plus 2 tablespoons all-purpose flour

Combine meat, tomatoes, onion, carrot, celery, allspice, 1 teaspoon salt, ¼ teaspoon pepper, and water in a small Dutch oven; bring to a boil. Reduce heat to low; cover and simmer 3 hours. Remove from heat; cool.

Strain broth, reserving meat and vegetables for other uses, if desired. Cover broth, and refrigerate overnight. Skim off and discard fat; strain broth through several layers of damp cheesecloth. Return broth to Dutch oven, and set aside.

Grind liver and crackers together; place in a small mixing bowl. Add eggs, flour, remaining salt, and pepper, mixing until well blended. Bring broth to a boil. Drop liver dumpling mixture by ½ teaspoonfuls into boiling broth. Cook 1 minute.

Ladle broth and dumplings into warm soup bowls, and serve immediately. Yield: about 1 quart.

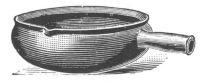

## BARLEY BROTH

4 pounds lamb neck bones
5 quarts water
½ pound barley
1 tablespoon salt
4 whole mace
1 cup chopped spinach
½ cup chopped fresh parsley
1 cup raisins

Combine neck bones and water in an 8-quart stockpot. Cover; cook over low heat 3 to 4 hours, bringing water slowly to a boil. Skim surface. Cover; simmer 1 hour.

Rinse barley, draining well. Add barley and salt to soup; stir well. Cover and simmer 3 hours. Stir in remaining ingredients; cover and simmer 1 hour.

Remove from heat; cool slightly. Strain through several layers of damp cheesecloth; discard bones, barley, mace, vegetables, and raisins. Cover and refrigerate broth overnight; remove and discard fat.

Reheat broth to serving temperature. Ladle into individual serving bowls. Yield: 3 quarts.

## AVGOLEMONO SOUP

2 quarts chicken broth
½ cup uncooked regular rice
4 eggs
¼ cup lemon juice

Place broth in a small Dutch oven; bring to a boil. Add rice. Reduce heat; cover and cook 20 minutes or until rice is tender. Remove from heat.

Place eggs in a small mixing bowl; beat with a wire whisk until light and foamy. Gradually add lemon juice, beating well; add 2 cups hot soup, beating constantly.

Add egg mixture to soup, beating constantly. Place over low heat, and bring just to a boil. (Do not boil because soup will curdle.)

Ladle soup into individual serving bowls; serve warm. Yield: about 2 quarts.

The versatility of the egg is nowhere more in evidence than when we use it in soup. We know egg emulsifies mayonnaise, thickens custard, and more. But in soups, it melds ingredients together smoothly and lends a slightly gelatinous, shiny quality. Egg as liaison does not cloud the broth as flour does. It has the clear quality of cornstarch, but the mouth-feel is quite different: not only silken to the tongue but noticeably rich. The Greeks have a word for their classic lemon soup enriched with an egg liaison: Avgolemono.

## EGG SOUP

2 eggs
¼ cup soft breadcrumbs
1 tablespoon chopped fresh parsley
⅛ teaspoon ground nutmeg
2 quarts chicken broth
1 (15-ounce) can asparagus spears, drained and chopped
1 (8.5-ounce) can green peas, drained

Combine eggs, breadcrumbs, parsley, and nutmeg in a large Dutch oven; beat well. Gradually stir in chicken broth; bring to a boil. Reduce heat to low; stir in asparagus and peas. Simmer, stirring constantly, 10 minutes or until vegetables are thoroughly heated. Ladle into individual soup bowls; serve immediately. Yield: about 3 quarts.

*Women of Milford, Delaware, attend demonstration of egg grading and packing, 1919.*

## LETTUCE SOUP

1 large head lettuce
1 quart chicken stock
1 thin slice onion
1 thin slice green pepper
1 small carrot, sliced
1 teaspoon salt
⅛ teaspoon white pepper
2 tablespoons all-purpose
   flour
¼ cup water
Cheese crackers (optional)

Shred lettuce; divide in half. Place one half of shredded lettuce, chicken stock, onion, green pepper, and carrot in a large Dutch oven, reserving remaining half of lettuce. Bring to a boil. Reduce heat; cover and simmer 30 to 40 minutes. Remove from heat, and let cool. Strain, reserving stock in Dutch oven; discard vegetables.

Add salt, pepper, and reserved uncooked lettuce to stock. Cover and simmer 30 minutes.

Combine flour and water; stir well to make a paste, and add to soup, stirring well. Cook 5 minutes. Serve warm in soup bowls with cheese crackers, if desired. Yield: 1½ quarts.

## MUSHROOM BROTH

1½ pounds fresh mushrooms,
   cleaned and finely chopped
½ teaspoon salt
¼ teaspoon pepper
1½ quarts water
¾ teaspoon beef broth and
   sauce concentrate
1 to 2 tablespoons dry
   vermouth

Combine mushrooms, salt, pepper, and water in a large Dutch oven. Place over medium heat, and bring to a boil. Reduce heat; cover and simmer 2 hours. Remove from heat, and cool slightly.

Strain mixture into a large saucepan; remove and reserve mushrooms for other uses. Place soup over medium heat, and stir in beef broth and sauce concentrate; heat thoroughly. Stir in vermouth, and serve soup warm or chilled as an appetizer. Yield: 1½ quarts.

## FRENCH ONION SOUP

6 medium-size yellow onions,
   thinly sliced and divided
¼ cup plus 2 tablespoons
   butter or margarine, divided
2 quarts beef broth, divided
6 (1-inch-thick) slices French
   bread
¾ cup grated Parmesan
   cheese

Combine one-third of onion slices and 2 tablespoons butter in a large skillet; sauté until onion is transparent. Transfer onions to a 5-quart casserole. Repeat procedure with remaining onion slices and butter.

Add 2 cups broth to onions in casserole, and bring to a boil. Reduce heat; cover and simmer 20 minutes or until onion is tender. Add remaining broth, and bring to a boil; remove soup from heat.

Cut each slice of French bread in half; toast each side. Arrange toasted bread on top of soup in casserole; sprinkle with cheese. Broil 8 inches from heating element 3 minutes or until cheese melts and becomes golden brown.

Ladle into individual soup bowls, placing a piece of toast in each bowl. Serve immediately. Yield: about 3 quarts.

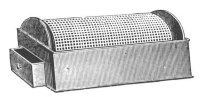

## HUGUENOT ONION SOUP

2 pounds onions, sliced
¼ cup butter or margarine
2 tablespoons all-purpose
   flour
1 teaspoon salt
1 quart water
12 beef-flavored bouillon
   cubes
1 quart milk
Croûtes
3 cups (12 ounces) shredded
   Swiss cheese, divided

Sauté onion in butter in a large Dutch oven 25 minutes or until tender. Stir in flour and salt. Add water and bouillon cubes, stirring well. Bring mixture to a boil. Reduce heat; cover and simmer 30 to 40 minutes. Gradually add 1 quart milk, stirring well. Heat thoroughly (do not boil).

Place soup in ovenproof bowls. Top each with 1 croûte and ¼ cup cheese. Bake at 325° for 5 minutes or until cheese melts. Serve immediately. Yield: 3 quarts.

### Croûtes:

1½ cups butter or margarine
1 large clove garlic, crushed
12 (1-inch-thick) slices
   French bread

Melt butter in a small saucepan; stir in garlic. Dip both sides of bread in garlic butter. Place bread on a baking sheet. Bake at 325° for 10 minutes on one side; turn and bake an additional 5 minutes. Yield: 12 slices.

---

*Lettuce Soup (front) and Egg Soup (page 33) will come as pleasant surprises to many.*

# INDIAN RIVER SOUP

**E**astern Florida's Indian River flows parallel to the Atlantic for 165 miles. Its length is taken up with resorts for hunting, fishing, and otherwise disporting oneself at vacation time. But the area has another claim to fame: citrus. So it is quite as natural to find orange juice in the soup there as it is to find salt pork in the turnip greens in Memphis. Indian River County lies within the valley and is widely known for its superb grapefruit.

1 (16-ounce) can Italian-style tomatoes, undrained
1 medium carrot, grated
1 small onion, finely chopped
1 small bay leaf
Rind of 1 lemon
6 whole peppercorns
3 cups chicken broth
½ cup vermouth or other dry, white wine
2 tablespoons sugar
¼ teaspoon salt
¼ teaspoon white pepper
⅓ cup orange juice
Rind of 1 orange, cut into very thin, ½-inch-long strips
2 tablespoons chopped fresh parsley

Combine tomatoes, carrot, onion, bay leaf, lemon rind, and peppercorns in a large saucepan; bring to a boil. Reduce heat; cover and simmer 8 minutes. Strain mixture, discarding pulp.

Return strained tomato mixture to saucepan; place over medium heat. Stir in broth, wine, and sugar; heat just to boiling. Stir in salt, pepper, and orange juice; heat thoroughly.

Ladle soup into individual bowls; garnish with orange rind and chopped parsley. Serve immediately as an appetizer. Yield: about 1 quart.

*Note:* Indian River Soup may be served chilled with 2 tablespoons vodka in each bowl.

*View at Rockledge on the Indian River in Florida, 1890.*

Florida State Archives

*Indian River Soup makes a refreshing appetizer served hot or chilled.*

## HOME-STYLE TOMATO SOUP

2 tablespoons butter or margarine
2 tablespoons all-purpose flour
1 (10½-ounce) can beef broth, undiluted
⅔ cup water
2 tablespoons finely chopped carrot
2 tablespoons finely chopped celery
2 tablespoons finely chopped onion
2 tablespoons finely chopped green pepper
1 bay leaf, crumbled
1 tablespoon dried parsley flakes
2 whole cloves
¼ teaspoon salt
¼ teaspoon pepper
2 (14½-ounce) cans whole tomatoes, undrained

Melt butter in a large saucepan; remove from heat, and stir in flour, broth, and water. Place over medium heat, and add carrot, celery, onion, green pepper, bay leaf, parsley flakes, cloves, salt, and pepper. Bring to a boil. Reduce heat; cover and simmer 25 minutes. Add tomatoes; cover and simmer an additional 20 minutes.

Strain mixture through several layers of cheesecloth; discard pulp. Cover and refrigerate remaining liquid overnight.

Skim off and discard layer of fat that rises to the surface. Place soup in a large saucepan over medium heat; bring to a boil, and serve immediately in individual bowls. Yield: 1 quart.

## QUICK TOMATO SOUP

¼ cup chopped onion
¼ cup chopped celery
1 tablespoon vegetable oil
1 quart tomato juice
1 teaspoon sugar
1 teaspoon salt
4 whole cloves
2 cups beef consommé
3 tablespoons lemon juice
Fresh watercress or parsley sprigs

Sauté onion and celery in oil in a medium saucepan until tender. Drain well. Add tomato juice, sugar, salt, and cloves. Cover and simmer 30 minutes. Remove from heat; cool slightly. Strain mixture; discard vegetables and whole spice. Cool to room temperature. Blot fat from surface of tomato mixture with paper towels.

Combine tomato mixture, consommé, and lemon juice in saucepan. Cook over low heat until thoroughly heated. Ladle soup into individual serving bowls. Garnish with watercress or parsley. Yield: 5 cups.

*Paring apples in an early American kitchen before mechanical parers appeared on the scene.*

## COLD APPLE SOUP

8 medium apples
2 cups apple juice
¼ cup lemon juice
2 tablespoons sugar
1 (3-inch) stick cinnamon
2 cups orange juice
2 cups half-and-half

Peel, core, and quarter 5 apples. Place in a 3-quart saucepan. Add apple juice, lemon juice, sugar, and cinnamon. Bring to a boil. Reduce heat; cover and simmer 15 minutes. Cover and refrigerate overnight. Remove and discard cinnamon.

Stir in orange juice and half-and-half. Pour one-third of mixture into container of an electric blender; process until smooth. Pour into a large serving bowl. Repeat with remaining mixture. Cover; chill thoroughly.

Shred remaining apples; stir into soup. Serve in chilled dessert bowls. Yield: 2½ quarts.

## COLD CANTALOUPE SOUP

2 medium cantaloupes, halved and seeded
1½ cups orange juice
¼ cup lime juice
1 tablespoon firmly packed brown sugar
1½ cups Sauterne or other sweet white wine
Fresh mint sprigs (optional)

Scoop out cantaloupe balls with a small melon baller to equal 2 cups; set aside. Combine remaining cantaloupe pulp, orange juice, lime juice, and brown sugar in container of an electric blender; process until smooth.

Combine cantaloupe mixture, melon balls, and wine in a large mixing bowl; cover and chill thoroughly. Stir well before serving in chilled bowls as a dessert soup. Garnish with mint, if desired. Yield: about 2 quarts.

## CHAMPAGNE-LEMON SOUP

1 (25.4-ounce) bottle brut champagne
½ cup sugar
Grated rind and juice of 1 medium lemon
8 egg yolks

Combine champagne, sugar, and lemon rind and juice in a large saucepan; stir well. Bring to a boil. Reduce heat to low; simmer 5 minutes.

Beat yolks in a small mixing bowl. Gradually stir one-fourth of hot mixture into yolks; add to remaining hot mixture, stirring constantly. Cook over medium heat, stirring constantly, until thickened. Ladle into individual soup bowls; serve warm as a dessert soup. Yield: 5 cups.

*Cold Cantaloupe (front), Cherry (page 40), and Apple Soups.*

*The dove displays the title of this 1872 Currier and Ives lithograph.*

## COLD CHERRY SOUP

3 cups plus 3 tablespoons
water, divided
1 cup sugar
1 (3-inch) stick cinnamon
3 cups pitted, dark sweet
cherries, drained
3 tablespoons all-purpose
flour
¾ cup Burgundy or other dry
red wine
¼ cup whipping cream

Combine 3 cups water, sugar, and cinnamon in a 2-quart saucepan; bring to a boil. Add cherries; cover and cook 10 minutes over medium heat. Remove cinnamon; discard.

Combine flour and remaining water in a small mixing bowl, stirring to blend; gradually stir into cherry mixture. Continue to cook over medium heat, stirring constantly, until mixture is slightly thickened. Remove from heat, and pour into a large glass mixing bowl. Cover and chill in refrigerator.

Before serving, stir in wine and whipping cream. Ladle soup into chilled bowls, and serve as a dessert. Yield: about 1½ quarts.

## COLD PAPAYA SOUP

1 medium papaya, peeled,
seeded, and cubed
¼ cup freshly squeezed lime
juice
½ cup sugar
½ cup Chablis or other dry
white wine

Place papaya in a small mixing bowl; pour lime juice over papaya, and toss gently. Set mixture aside.

Combine sugar and wine in a small saucepan; bring to a boil, and remove from heat. Pour over papaya mixture, and stir gently. Cover and refrigerate until thoroughly chilled. Serve soup in chilled dessert bowls. Yield: 2 cups.

## COLD PEACH SOUP

1½ cups water
¾ cup sugar
1 (3-inch) stick cinnamon,
   broken into pieces
4 whole cloves
2 tablespoons cornstarch
¼ cup cold water
1½ cups Chablis or other dry
   white wine
3 pounds fresh peaches,
   peeled, sliced, and divided
1 cup whipping cream,
   whipped
1 cup fresh blueberries

Combine 1½ cups water, sugar, cinnamon, and cloves in a small saucepan; place over medium heat, and bring to a boil. Reduce heat, and simmer 10 minutes, stirring occasionally.

Dissolve cornstarch in ¼ cup cold water, stirring well. Add to syrup in saucepan, stirring with a wire whisk; return mixture to a boil. Remove from heat, and stir in wine. Cool to room temperature. Remove cinnamon and cloves; discard. Set aside 1 cup syrup.

Combine 2 cups peach slices and remaining syrup in a large mixing bowl; set aside.

Place remaining peach slices and reserved 1 cup syrup in container of an electric blender; process until smooth. Combine with peach slices and syrup. Cover and chill thoroughly.

Ladle into chilled serving bowls. Garnish each serving with a dollop of whipped cream; sprinkle with blueberries. Serve immediately. Yield: 2½ quarts.

*Note*: Frozen peaches and blueberries may be substituted for fresh, if desired.

## COLD PEACH-ORANGE SOUP

2 pounds fresh peaches,
   peeled and sliced
1 tablespoon lemon juice
2½ cups water, divided
3 tablespoons instant tapioca
3 tablespoons sugar
Dash of salt
1 (6-ounce) can frozen orange
   juice concentrate, thawed
   and undiluted
1 orange, peeled and thinly
   sliced

Combine peaches and lemon juice in container of an electric blender; process until smooth. Set aside.

Combine 1 cup water, tapioca, sugar, and salt in a large saucepan. Bring to a boil, stirring frequently. Remove mixture from heat, and stir in remaining 1½ cups water, orange juice concentrate, and reserved pureed peach mixture. Cool to room temperature; cover and chill thoroughly.

Serve soup in chilled bowls; garnish each serving with orange slices. Yield: 1½ quarts.

*Note*: Cold Peach-Orange Soup may be served as an appetizer or dessert soup.

*Idyllic scene on a calendar card for September, 1890.*

# CHILLED RASPBERRY SOUP

3½ cups fresh raspberries, washed
3 cups water
1 cup rosé wine
¾ cup sugar
Pinch of salt
1 (8-ounce) carton commercial sour cream
Lime slices
Additional fresh raspberries

Place raspberries in container of an electric blender; process until smooth. Press through a sieve; discard seeds.

Pour pureed raspberries into a medium saucepan; stir in water, wine, sugar, and salt. Bring to a boil. Reduce heat; cover and simmer 5 minutes. Remove from heat; cool to room temperature. Add sour cream; blend well with a wire whisk. Cover; chill several hours.

Serve soup in chilled dessert bowls; garnish each serving with a lime slice and raspberry. Yield: about 2½ quarts.

# MARILYN'S STRAWBERRY SOUP

2 pints whole strawberries, hulled
2 cups orange juice
¾ cup honey
About ½ cup plain yogurt

Combine first 3 ingredients in container of an electric blender; process until smooth. Cover and chill thoroughly.

Ladle soup into chilled dessert bowls, and garnish each serving with a dollop of yogurt. Yield: 1½ quarts.

*Cool dessert: Marilyn's Strawberry Soup with garnish.*

# STRAWBERRY SOUP

2 pints whole strawberries, hulled
1¾ cups sifted powdered sugar
1 (8-ounce) carton commercial sour cream
1½ cups Burgundy or other dry red wine
1½ cups water
Additional whole strawberries
Additional sifted powdered sugar

Process 2 pints strawberries in a food mill, discarding excess pulp and seeds.

Combine the processed strawberries, 1¾ cups powdered sugar, and sour cream in a Dutch oven; beat well with a wire whisk. Gradually add wine and water, beating until mixture is well blended.

Cook over low heat, stirring constantly, until thoroughly heated and slightly thickened. (Do not boil.) Remove from heat; cool to room temperature. Cover and chill thoroughly.

Serve soup in chilled dessert bowls. Garnish each serving with a strawberry, and sprinkle with additional powdered sugar. Yield: about 2 quarts.

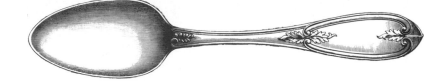

# DRIED FRUIT SOUP

¼ pound dried apples
¼ pound dried apricots
¼ pound dried prunes
1 quart cold water
½ cup sugar
1 (3-inch) stick cinnamon
1 tablespoon cornstarch
½ lemon, thinly sliced

Combine apples, apricots, prunes, and water in a large saucepan; let stand 1 hour.

Stir in sugar, and add cinnamon. Cover, and simmer over medium heat 40 minutes or until fruit is tender. Transfer fruit to a 1-quart serving dish, leaving liquid in saucepan; discard cinnamon.

Add cornstarch to liquid in saucepan, mixing well. Cook over medium heat, stirring occasionally, 15 minutes or until mixture begins to thicken. Add lemon slices, and pour over fruit in bowl. Cover and chill thoroughly. Serve in chilled bowls as a dessert soup. Yield: about 1 quart.

*Note*: Dried Fruit Soup may be served warm, if desired.

# SCANDINAVIAN FRUIT SOUP

2 (8-ounce) packages pitted prunes
1 cup golden raisins
¼ cup currants
Juice of 1 lemon
2 quarts plus 1 cup water, divided
½ cup pearl tapioca
1 (3-inch) stick cinnamon
1 (17-ounce) can peeled apricot halves, undrained
1 (16-ounce) can peach halves, undrained
1 (16-ounce) can pitted cherries, undrained
1 medium orange, thinly sliced
1 medium lemon, thinly sliced
Cognac

Combine prunes, raisins, currants, lemon juice, and 2 quarts water in a large Dutch oven; cover and let stand overnight.

Combine tapioca and remaining water; cover and let stand 1 hour. Drain well. Add drained tapioca and cinnamon to prune mixture. Cook over medium heat 30 minutes, stirring frequently. Add apricots, peaches, cherries, and orange and lemon slices; cook over low heat 30 minutes, stirring frequently. Remove from heat, and cool slightly. Remove cinnamon, and discard.

Spoon 1 teaspoon Cognac into each individual serving bowl; spoon soup into bowls, and serve immediately as an appetizer. Yield: 1 gallon.

*Note*: Scandinavian Fruit Soup may be chilled and served as a dessert soup.

*A colorful label for canned Moss Rose brand apricots.*

# CREAMS OF THE CROP

In between the rich, limpid liquid soup and the savory stew filled with every component of a well-balanced meal, there falls the cream soup and puree family. These are the real smoothies; for liquid they may contain bouillon or consommé and/or milk and cream. They are thickened by one of several methods and named for the major ingredient. Cream soup is much like a cream sauce, based on a cooked roux of flour and butter. In some cases, we thicken soup at the last minute with a flour-butter paste. It works, and leaves no raw flour flavor, which makes it an exception to the rule that flour must cook at least several minutes.

Old recipes for "white soups" usually contained a few almonds pounded to a paste, white stock of veal or chicken, and the aforementioned flour-butter added at the end. Alternative thickeners were and are soaked bread and crushed crackers. In some cases, egg yolks are added to the finished soup, imparting body and gloss as well as a luxurious, unctuous texture pleasing to the palate. In French cookery, the egg yolk addition is called a *liaison*. In those days before yesterday, when soup tureens were standard equipment, the yolks were beaten in the bottom of the tureen, and the soup poured gradually into the tureen and over the yolks.

Rich bisques made with seafood or poultry will contain, in most cases, both broth from the pre-cooked title ingredient and milk or cream. The meat is finely chopped and stirred back into the liquid. The food processor is of immense help in this operation; the seafood or chicken is easily reduced almost to a paste, if that is the texture desired.

Some soups thicken themselves: cheese, peanut butter, rice, barley, and potato, to name a few. The hair sieve, so laboriously used by good cooks of an earlier South, was supplanted first by the food mill, then by the electric blender and processor. One of the world's famous smooth soups is Vichyssoise, usually thought to have originated in France. The chef Louis Diat did come from there, but he invented the soup in 1910 at the Ritz Carlton in New York where he was chef for forty years. Among the good things of Southern cookery we find these lovely creamy-textured soups.

*Cream soups are more substantial than liquid-based ones, less so than our one-dish soup or stew meals: Cream of Chestnut (left), Cold Curried Squash (rear), and a cup of old-fashioned Rich Chicken Soup (right).*

# CHEESE AND NUT SPECIALTIES

## DRISKILL HOTEL CHEESE SOUP

½ cup finely chopped onion
½ cup thinly sliced carrot
½ cup thinly sliced celery
½ cup butter or margarine
¼ cup all-purpose flour
1½ tablespoons cornstarch
1 quart chicken broth
1 quart milk
2 cups (8 ounces) shredded sharp Cheddar cheese
⅛ teaspoon baking soda
½ teaspoon salt
¼ teaspoon pepper
2 tablespoons chopped fresh parsley

Sauté onion, carrot, and celery in butter in a large Dutch oven over low heat 10 minutes or until vegetables are tender.

Combine flour and cornstarch. Add to vegetables; cook over low heat, stirring constantly, until bubbly.

Combine broth and milk; gradually add to vegetable mixture. Cook over medium heat, stirring constantly, until mixture is thickened and bubbly. Add cheese, soda, salt, and pepper, stirring until cheese melts. Stir in parsley. Ladle soup into individual bowls, and serve immediately. Yield: about 2½ quarts.

When Col. J.L. Driskill opened his hotel in 1886, it was part of his dream to make Austin the beating heart of Texas. Enlarged to 180 rooms in 1930, the historic hotel has presided over major events from the Inaugural Ball of Gov. Sul Ross in 1887 to the dedication of the LBJ Suite in recent years. The Driskill is famous for its collection of Mexican artifacts.

*The Driskill Hotel in Austin, Texas, an elegant landmark since 1886. 1900 photo.*

*New Orleans Brewing Association offered three types of beer in a 1900s ad.*

## JALAPEÑO CHEESE SOUP

12 medium potatoes, peeled and sliced
3 (10¾-ounce) cans chicken broth, diluted
2 cups (8 ounces) shredded Monterey Jack cheese
1 large onion, sliced
1 small jalapeño pepper, halved
1 teaspoon butter or margarine
1 cup whipping cream, scalded
1 teaspoon salt
Avocado slices (optional)

Combine potatoes, chicken broth, cheese, onion, and jalapeño pepper in a large Dutch oven; bring to a boil. Reduce heat; simmer, uncovered, 30 minutes or until potatoes are tender. Remove from heat, and cool slightly.

Place 2 cups potato mixture in container of an electric blender; process until smooth, and set aside. Repeat procedure with remaining potato mixture. Return all pureed mixture to Dutch oven. Add butter, whipping cream, and salt; cook over low heat, stirring frequently, until butter melts and soup is thoroughly heated. Serve immediately in warm soup bowls; garnish with avocado slices, if desired. Yield: 3½ quarts.

## BEER CHEESE SOUP

¼ cup butter or margarine
⅓ cup all-purpose flour
3 cups chicken broth
2 cups milk
¼ teaspoon white pepper
1 cup beer
1 teaspoon Worcestershire sauce
¼ teaspoon hot sauce
3½ cups (14 ounces) shredded sharp Cheddar cheese
Croutons (optional)

Melt butter in a small Dutch oven over low heat; add flour, stirring until smooth. Cook 1 minute, stirring constantly. Gradually add broth and milk; cook over medium heat, stirring constantly, until thickened and bubbly. Stir in pepper.

Add next 3 ingredients, and bring to a boil, stirring frequently. Remove from heat; add cheese, and stir until melted. Ladle soup into individual bowls. Garnish each serving with croutons, if desired. Serve immediately. Yield: about 2 quarts.

## EMERGENCY CHEESE SOUP

¼ cup butter or margarine
¼ cup plus 2 tablespoons all-purpose flour
2 (10¾-ounce) cans chicken broth, undiluted
2 cups milk
¼ teaspoon white pepper
2 tablespoons chopped pimiento
¼ cup plus 2 tablespoons dry white wine
½ teaspoon Worcestershire sauce
¼ teaspoon hot pepper sauce
2 cups (8 ounces) shredded sharp Cheddar cheese

Melt butter in a heavy saucepan over low heat; add flour, stirring until smooth. Cook 1 minute, stirring constantly.

Gradually add broth and milk; cook over medium heat, stirring constantly, until thickened and bubbly. Stir in pepper. Add pimiento, white wine, Worcestershire sauce, and pepper sauce; stir well. Cook over medium heat, stirring frequently, until mixture is thoroughly heated. Remove from heat; add cheese, and stir until melted. Serve immediately. Yield: about 5 cups.

# BASIC CREAM SOUP HOW-TO

## CREAM SOUP

¼ cup butter or margarine
¼ cup all-purpose flour
2 cups chicken or beef broth or stock
2 cups whipping cream
Salt and white pepper to taste
Chopped fresh parsley (optional)

Melt butter in a heavy saucepan over low heat; add flour, stirring until smooth. Cook 1 minute, stirring constantly. Gradually add broth. Cook over medium heat, stirring constantly, until mixture is thickened. Reduce heat; gradually stir in whipping cream. Cook, stirring constantly, until mixture is thickened and smooth. Stir in salt and pepper.

Use Cream Soup as a foundation for a large variety of cream soups. Stir in 1½ cups of precooked meat, poultry, seafood, or vegetables. Cook over low heat, stirring constantly, until thoroughly heated. Yield: about 1½ quarts.

*Step 1—Melt butter in a heavy saucepan. Add flour, stirring until smooth. Cook for 1 minute, stirring constantly.*

*Step 2—Gradually add broth. Cook over medium heat, stirring constantly, until mixture is thickened.*

*Step 3—Stir in cream. Cook, stirring constantly, until mixture is thickened and smooth. Stir in seasonings.*

# CREAM OF PEANUT SOUP

1 cup thinly sliced celery
1 medium onion, finely
  chopped
¼ cup butter or margarine
2 tablespoons all-purpose
  flour
2 quarts chicken broth
1⅓ cups smooth peanut
  butter
1 cup half-and-half
⅛ teaspoon white pepper
Finely chopped peanuts

Sauté celery and onion in butter in a large Dutch oven over low heat 10 minutes or until tender. Remove from heat.

Add flour, stirring until smooth; stir in broth. Place over medium heat, and bring to a boil, stirring constantly. Add peanut butter, beating with a wire whisk until blended. Reduce heat; cover and simmer 15 minutes. Stir in half-and-half and pepper; heat just to boiling.

Ladle soup into individual serving bowls; garnish with chopped peanuts. Serve immediately. Yield: about 2 quarts.

# CREAM OF CHESTNUT SOUP

1½ pounds chestnuts
3 cups chicken broth
2 tablespoons butter or
  margarine
2 tablespoons all-purpose
  flour
3 cups milk
½ teaspoon salt
¼ teaspoon pepper
Chopped fresh parsley

Place chestnuts and water to cover in a small Dutch oven; bring to a boil. Cover and cook 20 minutes. Remove from heat; drain and cool.

Remove shells from chestnuts, and peel; coarsely chop chestnuts. Combine chestnuts and chicken broth in a medium saucepan. Place over medium heat, and bring to a boil. Reduce heat; cover and simmer 1 hour or until chestnuts are tender.

Place chestnut mixture in container of an electric blender; process on high speed until smooth.

Melt butter in a large saucepan over low heat; add flour, stirring until smooth. Cook 1 minute, stirring constantly. Gradually add milk; cook over medium heat, stirring constantly, until mixture is bubbly and begins to thicken. Remove from heat.

Add pureed chestnut mixture, salt, and pepper to cream sauce, beating with a wire whisk. Place over low heat; cook, stirring constantly, until thoroughly heated.

Ladle soup into individual serving bowls; garnish with chopped parsley. Serve immediately. Yield: about 1 quart.

*This young girl appears proud of her part in harvesting these peanut vines in this Virginia field, 1900.*

Rice cultivation began in this country in the seventeenth century, brought from its native Asiatic river deltas to the lowlands of the East Coast. Our rice is threshed and processed by machinery, but in some parts of the world, it is still flailed by hand or by beaters operated by treadmills. Unpolished brown rice contains more nutriments than white rice. Wild rice isn't rice; it is grain from an aquatic grass that grows in the North. As wild rice is expensive, it is often mixed with unpolished brown rice.

*"Methods of Treating Rice for Market," from* Leslie's Illustrated Newspaper, *1880.*

## CREAM OF RICE SOUP

1 quart milk
⅓ cup uncooked regular rice
6 whole cloves
1 medium onion, halved
¼ cup butter or margarine
¼ cup finely chopped fresh parsley
1½ teaspoons salt
⅓ cup hot milk (optional)

Combine 1 quart milk and rice in top of a double boiler. Place over simmering water; cover and cook 45 minutes or until rice is very soft.

Pour rice into container of an electric blender; process until smooth. Return rice to top of double boiler. Place 3 cloves in each onion half; add to rice. Cover; cook 15 minutes. Remove and discard onion. Remove boiler from heat; stir in butter, parsley, and salt. Stir in hot milk for a thinner soup, if desired. Ladle into soup bowls. Yield: about 1 quart.

## CREAM OF WILD RICE SOUP

1 small onion, chopped
1 small green pepper, seeded and chopped
1 stalk celery, chopped
¼ cup sliced fresh mushrooms
¼ cup butter or margarine
½ cup all-purpose flour
1 quart hot chicken broth
2 cups cooked wild rice
Salt and pepper to taste
½ cup evaporated milk
1 tablespoon Chablis or other dry white wine

Sauté first 4 ingredients in butter in a small Dutch oven until tender. Add flour; stir well. Gradually add broth, stirring constantly. Stir in rice and salt and pepper. Cook, uncovered, over medium heat until thoroughly heated. Remove from heat; stir in milk and wine. Ladle into individual soup bowls. Yield: 1½ quarts.

*Cream of Wild Rice Soup rates high on flavor and texture.*

# SEAFOOD AND POULTRY DELIGHTS

*Shell collectors with baskets at Pablo Beach, Florida, c.1900.*

## CLAM BISQUE

2 cups clams, undrained
1 quart chicken broth
½ cup uncooked regular rice
1 sprig fresh parsley
1 bay leaf
1 cup whipping cream
½ teaspoon salt
¼ teaspoon pepper

Boil clams in clam liquid 5 minutes. Place in container of an electric blender; process until finely chopped.

Combine chopped clams, chicken broth, rice, parsley, and bay leaf in a large Dutch oven; bring to a boil. Reduce heat; cover and cook 25 minutes or until rice is tender. Strain mixture through a sieve into a large bowl; set broth aside.

Remove and discard parsley and bay leaf. Process mixture through a food mill; stir into reserved broth. Strain broth mixture a second time; discard any remaining clam and rice particles in sieve.

Combine strained broth mixture, whipping cream, salt, and pepper in a large Dutch oven; cook over low heat, stirring frequently, until thoroughly heated. (Do not boil.) Ladle into individual soup bowls; serve immediately. Yield: about 1 quart.

## CRAB BISQUE

½ cup peeled and finely chopped cucumber
½ cup finely chopped onion
¼ cup plus 2 tablespoons butter or margarine
½ cup all-purpose flour
1 quart hot Fish Stock (page 12)
1 quart hot half-and-half
1 pound lump or flake crabmeat, finely chopped
½ teaspoon salt
¼ teaspoon white pepper
1 tablespoon Rhine wine
Additional cucumber slices (optional)
Hot French bread (optional)

Sauté cucumber and onion in butter in a large Dutch oven until tender. Add flour, stirring until smooth. Cook 5 minutes, stirring constantly. Gradually add fish stock; cook over medium heat, stirring constantly, until thickened and bubbly. Stir in half-and-half, crabmeat, salt, and pepper. Remove from heat; cover and chill thoroughly.

Stir in wine just before serving. Serve chilled in individual soup bowls. Garnish with cucumber slices, and serve with French bread, if desired. Yield: about 2½ quarts.

## SPINACH AND CRABMEAT SOUP

2 (10-ounce) packages frozen chopped spinach
1 medium onion, sliced
1½ quarts chicken broth, divided
¼ cup plus 2 tablespoons butter or margarine
2 tablespoons all-purpose flour
¼ teaspoon salt
⅛ teaspoon white pepper
2 cups half-and-half
1 pound lump crabmeat
½ teaspoon ground nutmeg

Cook spinach according to package directions, with onion slices. Drain mixture. Place mixture and 2 cups chicken broth in container of an electric blender; process until smooth.

Melt butter in a large Dutch oven over low heat; add flour, salt, and pepper, stirring until smooth. Cook 1 minute, stirring constantly. Gradually add remaining chicken broth; bring to a boil, stirring constantly. Stir in spinach mixture; simmer, uncovered, over low heat 10 minutes. Add half-and-half and crabmeat, stirring well. Heat thoroughly. (Do not boil.) Stir in nutmeg. Ladle into soup bowls. Yield: 3 quarts.

*Best foot forward for company: Spinach and Crabmeat Soup.*

Beaufort County Library

An 1864 view of Bay Street in Beaufort, South Carolina, shows the Post Office, Adam's Express Co., and the Beaufort Hotel.

## OYSTER BISQUE

3 (12-ounce) containers Standard oysters, undrained
1 quart milk, divided
½ cup chopped celery
½ green pepper, chopped
3 tablespoons butter or margarine
3 tablespoons all-purpose flour
1 teaspoon salt
½ teaspoon white pepper
1 tablespoon Worcestershire sauce

Combine oysters, 1 cup milk, celery, and green pepper in container of an electric blender; process until smooth. Set aside.

Melt butter in a small Dutch oven over low heat; add flour, stirring until smooth. Cook 1 minute, stirring constantly. Gradually add remaining milk; cook over medium heat, stirring constantly, until thickened and bubbly. Stir in salt and pepper. Gradually stir in reserved oyster mixture. Continue to cook over medium heat until thoroughly heated. (Do not boil.) Stir in Worcestershire sauce. Ladle into individual soup bowls; serve immediately. Yield: about 2 quarts.

## BEAUFORT CREAM OF CRAB SOUP

1 cup finely chopped onion
1 tablespoon butter or margarine
1 chicken-flavored bouillon cube
1 cup hot water
1 quart half-and-half
1 tablespoon finely chopped fresh parsley
½ teaspoon salt
½ teaspoon celery salt
⅛ teaspoon ground mace
⅛ teaspoon white pepper
Dash of red pepper
1 pound lump crabmeat
2 tablespoons all-purpose flour
2 tablespoons water
¼ cup dry sherry

Sauté onion in butter in a large Dutch oven until tender. Dissolve bouillon cube in hot water; gradually add bouillon and half-and-half to sautéed onion, stirring well. Stir in parsley, salt, celery salt, mace, pepper, and crabmeat; simmer over low heat 15 minutes, stirring constantly.

Combine flour and 2 tablespoons water, stirring to make a smooth paste. Stir paste into soup, and cook until slightly thickened. Remove from heat; stir in sherry. Ladle into individual soup bowls, and serve immediately. Yield: 2 quarts.

## CREAM OF LOBSTER SOUP

1 quart milk, scalded
3 tablespoons fine, dry breadcrumbs
¼ cup butter or margarine
¼ cup all-purpose flour
1 quart whipping cream
1½ cups chopped, cooked lobster
½ cup sherry
¾ teaspoon salt
½ teaspoon white pepper

Combine milk and breadcrumbs in a small mixing bowl; let stand 20 minutes. Set mixture aside.

Melt butter in a small Dutch oven over low heat; add flour, stirring until smooth. Cook 1 minute, stirring constantly. Gradually add milk mixture and whipping cream; cook over medium heat, stirring constantly, until slightly thickened. Stir in remaining ingredients. Continue to cook over medium heat until thoroughly heated. Serve immediately in individual soup bowls. Yield: about 2 quarts.

An often-quoted recipe from Mary Randolph's 1824 *The Virginia Housewife* is for oyster soup. She used two quarts of oysters to make a soup base, strained the liquid and started afresh with another quart of oysters! Mrs. Porter, in *New Southern Cookery Book*, 1871, observed that oysters should never be boiled; it toughens them.

## JEFFERSON DAVIS' OYSTER SOUP

1 quart milk
1 tablespoon butter or margarine, melted
1 tablespoon all-purpose flour
1 cup finely chopped celery
½ teaspoon salt
¼ teaspoon white pepper
⅛ teaspoon red pepper (optional)
3 (12-ounce) containers Standard oysters, undrained

Scald milk in a large Dutch oven. Combine melted butter and flour, stirring until smooth; add to hot milk, stirring well. Add celery, and cook over medium heat 10 minutes, stirring constantly. (Do not boil.) Stir in salt, white pepper, and red pepper, if desired.

Add oysters and liquid, stirring well. Reduce heat to low, and continue cooking, stirring constantly, until mixture is thoroughly heated and oyster edges curl. Ladle into individual soup bowls. Serve immediately. Yield: 2 quarts.

Jefferson Davis, President of the Confederacy, first married the daughter of Col. Zachary Taylor; she lived only three months. Ten years later in 1845 Davis married Varina Howell, pictured above.

## BAKED OYSTER SOUP

1½ quarts half-and-half
2 tablespoons butter or margarine
12 saltine crackers, crushed
¼ cup finely chopped celery
½ teaspoon salt
¼ teaspoon pepper
2 (12-ounce) containers Standard oysters, drained
Oyster crackers (optional)

Scald half-and-half in a large Dutch oven. Add butter, cracker crumbs, celery, salt, and pepper; mix well. Add oysters, a few at a time, to half-and-half mixture. Heat thoroughly. (Do not boil.) Pour into a 3-quart casserole. Bake, uncovered, at 350° for 30 minutes, stirring mixture at 15 minute intervals. Bake an additional 20 minutes, without stirring, to brown top. Ladle into individual soup bowls, and serve immediately. Serve with oyster crackers, if desired. Yield: about 2½ quarts.

*This rich Baked Oyster Soup contains generous amounts of cream.*

# SHRIMP BISQUE

1½ quarts water
1½ pounds uncooked medium
   shrimp, peeled and deveined
1 large onion, chopped
2 stalks celery, quartered
2 cloves garlic, chopped
¼ cup chopped fresh parsley,
   divided
Grated rind of ½ lemon
1 tablespoon lemon juice
½ teaspoon dried whole
   thyme
¼ cup minced green pepper
2 tablespoons chopped green
   onion
1 clove garlic, chopped
¼ cup butter or margarine,
   divided
½ cup French bread crumbs
1 egg yolk
1¼ teaspoons salt, divided
¾ teaspoon pepper, divided
1 teaspoon paprika
2 tablespoons all-purpose
   flour
½ teaspoon red pepper
1 quart whipping cream

Place water in a large Dutch oven; bring to a boil. Stir in shrimp, and cook over high heat 2 minutes. Remove shrimp from cooking liquid with a slotted spoon, reserving cooking liquid in Dutch oven; rinse shrimp with cold water. Set shrimp aside in refrigerator.

Add onion, celery, 2 cloves chopped garlic, 3 tablespoons parsley, lemon rind, juice, and thyme to shrimp cooking liquid. Cover and cook over medium heat 2 hours, stirring occasionally. Remove from heat, and cool slightly.

Finely chop 1¼ cups reserved cooked shrimp; set aside in refrigerator. Combine remaining reserved shrimp and 2 cups shrimp cooking liquid in container of an electric blender; process until smooth. Repeat procedure with remaining shrimp cooking liquid and vegetables. Return pureed mixture to Dutch oven; set aside.

Sauté green pepper, green onion, remaining parsley, and 1 clove chopped garlic in 2 tablespoons butter; remove from heat, and cool slightly. Stir in

*St. Augustine Harbor photographed by F.B. Johnston, c.1930.*

chopped shrimp, bread crumbs, egg yolk, ¼ teaspoon salt, and ¼ teaspoon pepper; shape shrimp mixture into 12 balls. Place shrimp balls on a greased baking sheet, and sprinkle with paprika. Bake at 350° for 10 minutes. Set shrimp balls aside and keep warm.

Melt remaining butter in a small skillet over low heat; add flour and cook, stirring constantly, until roux is the color of a copper penny. Stir roux, remaining salt and pepper, and red pepper into bisque; cook over low heat until bisque is thoroughly heated. Remove from heat, and stir in whipping cream.

Place shrimp balls in individual soup bowls; ladle bisque over balls. Serve immediately. Yield: 2 quarts.

## CREAM OF SHRIMP SOUP

2 pounds uncooked medium
  shrimp, peeled, deveined,
  and halved
½ cup butter or margarine
¼ teaspoon garlic powder
¼ cup plus 2 tablespoons
  all-purpose flour
3 cups whipping cream
3 cups chicken broth
1 bay leaf
1½ teaspoons salt
½ teaspoon white pepper
2 tablespoons chopped chives

Sauté shrimp in butter and garlic powder in a large Dutch oven 5 minutes; remove shrimp with a slotted spoon, and set aside. Reserve pan drippings.

Add flour to pan drippings; stir until smooth. Cook 1 minute, stirring constantly. Gradually add whipping cream, broth, and bay leaf; cook over medium heat, stirring constantly, until thickened and bubbly. Stir in salt, pepper, and chives. Remove and discard bay leaf.

Ladle soup into individual serving bowls; serve warm. Yield: 2 quarts.

## CHILLED SHRIMP SOUP

1 quart water
¼ teaspoon liquid crab and
  shrimp boil
1 pound uncooked medium
  shrimp, peeled and deveined
¼ cup butter or margarine
¼ cup all-purpose flour
1 tablespoon minced onion
¼ cup tomato paste
1 cup half-and-half
½ teaspoon salt
¼ teaspoon pepper
¼ teaspoon curry powder
Dash of red pepper
Cherry tomato slices
  (optional)
Whole boiled shrimp, peeled
  (optional)

Place water and crab and shrimp boil in a medium Dutch oven; bring to a boil. Stir in 1 pound uncooked shrimp, and cook over high heat 2 minutes. Remove shrimp from cooking liquid with a slotted spoon, reserving 3½ cups cooking liquid; rinse shrimp with cold water. Finely chop shrimp; cover and set aside in refrigerator.

Melt butter in a large saucepan over low heat; add flour, stirring until smooth. Cook 1 minute, stirring constantly. Gradually add reserved shrimp cooking liquid; bring to a boil. Cook over high heat, stirring frequently, 15 minutes. Reduce heat, and add chopped shrimp and onion. Simmer 10 minutes.

Stir in tomato paste, half-and-half, salt, pepper, curry powder, and red pepper; simmer an additional 3 minutes, stirring frequently. Remove from heat, and cool to room temperature. Cover and chill.

Serve soup in chilled soup bowls; garnish with tomato slices and whole peeled shrimp, if desired. Yield: 4½ cups.

*Cans of Grand Isle brand fresh shrimp out of Louisiana carried an attention-getting label.*

IF THE LINING INSIDE THIS CAN SHOWS ANY DISCOLORED SPOTS, THE QUALITY OF THE SHRIMP IS IN NO WAY

GRAND ISLE
BRAND

EXCELLENT FOR ALL KIND
OF COLD DISHES ESPECIALL
FOR CHAFING DISH.

DRY PACK
CONTENTS 5 OZS.

FRESH
SHRIMP

PACKED BY
GRAND ISLE CANNING C
WESTWEGO, LA.

# CHARLESTON WHITE BISQUE

6 blanched almonds
1 tablespoon all-purpose flour
5 quarts plus ¼ cup water, divided
1 (5-pound) hen, cut up
3 blades whole mace
1 quart whipping cream, divided
½ cup soft breadcrumbs
½ teaspoon salt
¼ teaspoon white pepper
2 cups hot milk
Paprika (optional)

Pound almonds to make a paste; set aside. Combine flour and ¼ cup water to form a smooth paste; set aside.

Combine hen, mace, and remaining water in a large stockpot; bring to a boil. Reduce heat; cover and simmer 1 hour or until hen is tender. Remove hen from broth and cool, reserving broth. Bone breasts and wings, and cut meat into bite-size pieces. Reserve remaining chicken for use in other recipes. Combine chicken pieces, almond paste, and 2 cups whipping cream in container of an electric blender; process until smooth. Set aside.

Combine 1 quart reserved broth, remaining whipping cream, breadcrumbs, and pureed chicken mixture in a large Dutch oven. Bring to a boil. Stir in reserved flour mixture, salt, pepper, and hot milk. Heat thoroughly (do not boil). Serve immediately in individual soup bowls. Sprinkle each serving with paprika, if desired. Yield: about 3 quarts.

In 1901, when *The Original Picayune's Creole Cook Book* was first copyrighted, it defined bisque as ". . . a soup made of shellfish. It is red in color, such as Crawfish Bisque, the shells of which are boiled and mashed and pounded and strained and added to the soup stock. A Lobster Bisque may be prepared in the same way. . . ." The definition still holds. Although the term is used more loosely today, "bisques" made of other meats are not true bisques. Nonetheless, they can be lovely soups.

*1869 Currier and Ives lithograph:* The Poultry Yard.

*Soup cookery is not usually a dressy occupation . . . unless we are posing for an advertisement.*

## CREAM OF CHICKEN SOUP

1 (4½- to 5-pound) hen, quartered
1 gallon water
1 medium onion, quartered
1 stalk celery, halved
½ cup uncooked regular rice
2 tablespoons chopped fresh parsley
2 teaspoons salt
½ teaspoon pepper
2 cups milk
¼ cup all-purpose flour

Combine hen, water, onion, and celery in a large stockpot; bring to a boil. Reduce heat; simmer, uncovered, 3 hours.

Remove hen from broth; bone and chop meat. Set white meat aside; reserve dark meat for use in other recipes. Strain broth, and discard vegetables. (Chicken and broth may be refrigerated overnight.) Skim off and discard excess fat from broth.

Return broth to stockpot; bring to a boil. Stir in rice, parsley, salt, and pepper. Reduce heat; cover and cook 20 minutes or until rice is tender.

Gradually add milk to flour, stirring constantly, until smooth. Stir flour mixture and white meat into rice mixture. Cook over medium heat, stirring frequently, until thickened and thoroughly heated. Serve immediately in warm soup bowls. Yield: about 2½ quarts.

## RICH CHICKEN SOUP

⅓ cup butter or margarine
¾ cup all-purpose flour
1½ quarts chicken stock
1 cup milk
1 cup whipping cream
½ teaspoon salt
½ teaspoon white pepper
2 cups finely diced cooked chicken
Chopped fresh celery leaves

Melt butter in a small Dutch oven over low heat; add flour, stirring until smooth. Cook 1 minute, stirring constantly. Gradually add chicken stock, milk, and whipping cream; cook over medium heat, stirring constantly, until thickened and bubbly. Stir in salt and pepper. Add diced chicken to Dutch oven; cook over medium heat, stirring constantly, 3 minutes or until thoroughly heated. Ladle soup into individual bowls; top each with chopped celery leaves. Serve immediately. Yield: about 2 quarts.

# VEGETABLES FROM EVERY SEASON

### CREAM OF ARTICHOKE SOUP

½ cup chopped onion
½ cup chopped celery
1 tablespoon butter or margarine
2 (14-ounce) cans artichoke hearts, undrained
3 tablespoons all-purpose flour
1 quart chicken broth
1 quart milk
½ teaspoon salt
Dash of red pepper

Sauté chopped onion and celery in butter in a large skillet until vegetables are tender. Place vegetables and artichoke hearts in container of an electric blender; process until smooth.

Place flour in a large Dutch oven. Gradually add chicken broth, stirring until smooth. Cook over medium heat, stirring constantly, until thickened and bubbly. Stir in artichoke mixture; cook over medium heat until bubbly. Add milk, salt, and pepper; heat thoroughly. (Do not boil.) Serve warm or chilled in individual soup bowls. Yield: 2½ quarts.

### CREAM OF ASPARAGUS SOUP

2 pounds fresh asparagus spears
1 quart chicken stock
¼ cup butter or margarine
¼ cup all-purpose flour
2 cups milk
½ teaspoon salt
¼ teaspoon pepper

Snap off tough ends of asparagus. Remove scales from stalks. Chop asparagus.

Combine asparagus and chicken stock in a large saucepan; bring to a boil. Reduce heat; cover and simmer 6 minutes or until crisp-tender. Remove from heat; set aside.

Melt butter in a small Dutch oven over low heat; add flour, stirring until smooth. Cook 1 minute, stirring constantly. Gradually add milk; cook over medium heat, stirring constantly, until thickened and bubbly. Stir in salt and pepper.

Stir in chicken stock and asparagus. Cook over medium heat until hot. Ladle into individual soup bowls; serve warm or chilled. Yield: 2 quarts.

### CREAM OF BROCCOLI SOUP

1 (10-ounce) package frozen broccoli
1 medium onion, chopped
3 tablespoons butter or margarine
¼ cup chopped fresh parsley
¼ cup all-purpose flour
2 cups chicken broth, divided
2 cups half-and-half
2 tablespoons lemon juice
¾ teaspoon salt
¼ teaspoon garlic powder
½ teaspoon lemon-pepper seasoning
⅛ teaspoon red pepper
⅛ teaspoon ground nutmeg (optional)
Additional chopped fresh parsley

Cook broccoli according to package directions; drain well, and set aside.

Sauté onion in butter in a large saucepan until tender; add reserved broccoli and ¼ cup parsley, and cook 3 minutes, stirring constantly. Sprinkle flour evenly over broccoli mixture; cook 2 minutes, stirring constantly.

Transfer broccoli mixture to container of an electric blender; add 1 cup chicken broth, and process until smooth.

Return mixture to saucepan; add remaining broth, half-and-half, lemon juice, salt, garlic powder, lemon-pepper seasoning, pepper, and nutmeg, if desired, stirring well. Cook over medium heat 5 minutes or until thoroughly heated.

Ladle soup into individual serving bowls; garnish with additional chopped parsley. Serve warm. Yield: about 1 quart.

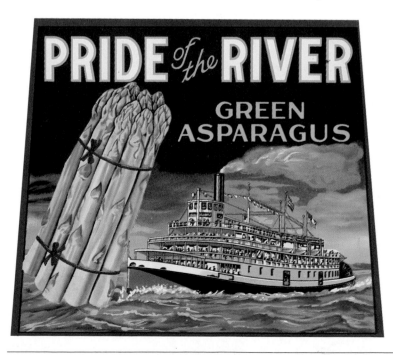

*Liebig Co. 1880s ad for extract of meat shows kitchen stocked with plenty of fresh ingredients for soup.*

SEE THAT THE LABEL BEARS
THE SIGNATURE IN BLUE INK THUS
SEE THAT THE LABEL BEARS
THE SIGNATURE IN BLUE INK THU

# CREAM OF CARROT SOUP

2½ cups water
2 chicken-flavored bouillon cubes
1 beef-flavored bouillon cube
5 large carrots, scraped and thinly sliced
5 stalks celery, thinly sliced
1 small potato, peeled and diced
1 small onion, chopped
1 tablespoon chopped fresh parsley
¼ teaspoon salt
¼ teaspoon pepper
3 tablespoons butter or margarine
1 tablespoon plus 1½ teaspoons cornstarch
¼ teaspoon dried whole basil
¼ teaspoon dried whole marjoram
¼ teaspoon dried whole thyme
½ teaspoon Angostura bitters
2 cups milk
1½ cups commercial sour cream, divided
Chopped chives

Combine water, bouillon cubes, carrots, celery, potato, onion, parsley, salt, and pepper in a medium Dutch oven; place over medium heat, and bring to a boil. Reduce heat; cover and simmer 40 minutes or until vegetables are tender.

Transfer vegetables and cooking liquid to container of an electric blender; process until smooth. Add butter, cornstarch, basil, marjoram, thyme, and Angostura bitters; process until well blended. Return mixture to Dutch oven.

Stir in milk; cook over low heat, stirring constantly, 5 minutes or until mixture thickens. Add 1 cup sour cream; mix well.

Ladle soup into individual serving bowls. Garnish with remaining sour cream and chopped chives. Serve warm. Yield: 2 quarts.

*Burpee's Best-Early Cauliflower, accurately engraved from a photograph, 1893.*

# CAULIFLOWER SOUP

½ cup chopped onion
1 tablespoon butter or margarine
1½ quarts chicken broth, divided
½ teaspoon curry powder
1½ cups cooked regular rice
1 medium head cauliflower, broken into small flowerets
1 cup whipping cream
1 teaspoon salt
½ teaspoon pepper

Sauté onion in butter in a medium saucepan until tender. Add 2 cups chicken broth and curry powder; bring to a boil. Reduce heat; simmer, uncovered, 15 minutes. Remove from heat; stir in rice.

Pour rice mixture into container of an electric blender, and process until smooth.

Combine cauliflower and remaining chicken broth in a large Dutch oven; bring to a boil. Reduce heat; simmer, uncovered, 15 minutes or until tender. Stir in rice mixture, whipping cream, salt, and pepper. Serve in individual soup bowls. Yield: 2 quarts.

# CREAM OF CORN SOUP

2 (17-ounce) cans cream-style corn
10 cups milk, divided
1½ cups chopped onion
6 tablespoons butter or margarine
6 tablespoons all-purpose flour
2 teaspoons salt
½ teaspoon white pepper
Paprika

Combine corn and 1 cup milk in container of an electric blender; process until smooth. Set aside.

Sauté onion in butter in a large Dutch oven until tender. Add flour; cook 1 minute, stirring constantly. Gradually add remaining milk; cook over medium heat, stirring constantly, until thickened and bubbly. Stir in salt and pepper. Gradually add reserved corn mixture, stirring well. Continue to cook, uncovered, over medium heat until thoroughly heated. Ladle into individual soup bowls; sprinkle with paprika, and serve immediately. Yield: about 2 quarts.

*Cream of Corn Soup is especially savory when served with crisp brown corn sticks and butter.*

## CREAM OF EGGPLANT SOUP

2 small eggplant, peeled, seeded, and diced
1 large potato, peeled and diced
1½ cups finely chopped celery
1½ cups finely chopped onion
¼ cup butter or margarine
Pinch of ground thyme
Pinch of dried whole basil
1 teaspoon curry powder
1½ quarts chicken broth
2 cups warm whipping cream
Salt and pepper to taste

Sauté eggplant, potato, celery, and onion in butter in a large Dutch oven until tender. Stir in thyme, basil, and curry powder; let cool. Transfer vegetable mixture to container of an electric blender; process until smooth.

Return pureed mixture to Dutch oven. Stir in chicken broth; bring to a boil. Reduce heat; cover and simmer 45 minutes. Remove from heat; add warm whipping cream, stirring well. Stir in salt and pepper. Ladle into individual soup bowls; serve immediately. Yield: 3 quarts.

## CREAM OF CUCUMBER SOUP

1 large cucumber, peeled and diced (about 2 cups)
¼ cup chopped onion
¼ cup chopped celery
¼ cup chopped green pepper
3 sprigs fresh parsley
3 tablespoons butter or margarine
2 tablespoons all-purpose flour
1 cup chicken broth
1 cup half-and-half
½ teaspoon salt
¼ teaspoon white pepper
Fresh dillweed sprigs

Combine cucumber, onion, celery, green pepper, and parsley in container of an electric blender; process until smooth. Set mixture aside.

Melt butter in a large saucepan over medium heat; add flour, and cook 1 minute, stirring constantly. Add chicken broth and half-and-half; cook, stirring constantly, until mixture is thickened and bubbly. Stir in salt and pepper.

Add reserved cucumber mixture to sauce; cook over medium heat, stirring frequently, until thoroughly heated.

Ladle soup into individual serving bowls; garnish each serving with dillweed, and serve warm. Soup may also be served chilled. Yield: about 1 quart.

*Mushrooms are a soup-maker's friend: Seafood-Mushroom Soup (front) and Cream of Mushroom Soup in a cup.*

## SEAFOOD-MUSHROOM SOUP

¼ cup plus 3 tablespoons
  butter or margarine, divided
½ cup all-purpose flour
3 cups half-and-half
2 cups milk
1 cup sliced fresh
  mushrooms
1½ cups chopped, cooked
  seafood (cod, haddock,
  shrimp, lobster, or
  combination of seafood)
1 hard-cooked egg, finely
  chopped
1½ teaspoons salt
¼ teaspoon white pepper
½ teaspoon grated lemon rind
½ teaspoon sugar
¼ cup cream sherry
3 hard-cooked egg yolks,
  grated
2 tablespoons chopped chives
  (optional)

Melt ¼ cup plus 2 tablespoons butter in top of a double boiler over simmering water; add flour, and stir with a wire whisk until smooth. Cook 1 minute, stirring constantly. Gradually add half-and-half and milk. Cook over simmering water, stirring constantly, until thickened and bubbly.

Sauté mushrooms in remaining butter in a small skillet until tender. Stir sautéed mushrooms into sauce. Add seafood, chopped egg, salt, pepper, lemon rind, and sugar; stir well. Cook over simmering water 25 minutes, stirring occasionally.

Add sherry; cook 5 minutes. Pour soup into individual serving bowls; garnish with grated egg yolk and chives, if desired. Yield: 1½ quarts.

## CREAM OF MUSHROOM SOUP

½ pound fresh mushrooms,
  cleaned and divided
3 cups water
½ small onion, thinly sliced
½ teaspoon salt
¼ cup butter or margarine
¼ cup all-purpose flour
1 cup milk
½ cup whipping cream
¼ teaspoon paprika
Dash of red pepper

Coarsely chop mushrooms to equal ½ cup; set aside.

Combine remaining mushrooms, water, onion, and salt in a large saucepan; bring to a boil. Reduce heat; cook, uncovered, 30 minutes. Transfer to container of an electric blender; process until smooth. Set aside.

Melt butter in a large saucepan over low heat; add reserved chopped mushrooms, and sauté 3 minutes. Add flour; cook 1 minute, stirring constantly. Gradually add milk; cook, stirring constantly, until mixture is thickened and bubbly.

Add pureed mushroom mixture, stirring well; cook until thoroughly heated. Stir in whipping cream, paprika, and pepper just before serving.

Ladle soup into individual serving bowls. Serve warm. Yield: about 1½ quarts.

## GREEN PEA SOUP

1 quart chicken broth
1 teaspoon salt
¼ teaspoon pepper
1 quart shelled fresh green peas
1 cup finely chopped celery
1 cup finely chopped onion
2 tablespoons butter or margarine
1 tablespoon all-purpose flour
½ cup whipping cream
2 tablespoons chopped fresh parsley

Combine chicken broth, salt, and pepper in a large Dutch oven; bring to a rolling boil. Add shelled peas, celery, and onion; return to a boil. Cook, uncovered, 20 minutes or until peas are tender. Strain through a food mill into a large bowl. Process vegetables, discarding vegetable pulp. Return vegetable mixture to Dutch oven, and set aside.

Melt butter in a heavy saucepan over low heat; add flour, stirring until smooth. Cook 1 minute, stirring constantly. Gradually add whipping cream; cook over medium heat, stirring constantly, until thickened and bubbly.

Gradually stir reserved vegetable mixture into cream sauce. Heat thoroughly. (Do not boil.) Serve immediately in individual soup bowls; garnish with chopped parsley. Yield: about 1½ quarts.

## SPLIT PEA SOUP

1½ cups dried split green peas
4½ cups cold water
1 large onion, sliced
1 cup diced celery
½ pound cooked ham, diced
1½ teaspoons salt
½ teaspoon pepper
3 cups milk

Combine peas and water in a medium Dutch oven. Cover and let soak overnight.

Place Dutch oven over medium heat; add onion, celery, ham, salt, and pepper. Bring to a boil. Reduce heat; cover and simmer 3 hours, stirring occasionally.

Add milk; heat just to boiling, stirring occasionally.

Ladle soup into individual serving bowls; serve warm. Yield: 2 quarts.

*Appealing label from can of Thurber & Company's peas, c.1885.*

# GREEN ONION SOUP

3  bunches green onions,
   finely chopped
3  tablespoons butter or
   margarine
3  tablespoons all-purpose
   flour
1½ cups chicken broth
1½ cups half-and-half
½  cup milk
½  cup vermouth
½  cup water
½  teaspoon salt
¼  teaspoon white pepper
¼  teaspoon hot sauce

Sauté green onion in butter in a large Dutch oven until tender; add flour, and stir well. Cook 1 minute, stirring constantly. Gradually add broth, half-and-half, milk, vermouth, and water; cook over low heat, stirring constantly, until slightly thickened and bubbly. Add salt, pepper, and hot sauce; stir well.

Bring to a boil. Reduce heat; simmer, uncovered, 30 minutes. Serve in warm soup bowls. Yield: 1½ quarts.

The variety of recipes in this chapter makes it apparent that nearly any vegetable can be transformed into a delectable soup. Creativity begins where recipes leave off. Experimentation is the key. With some good broth, some cream, and a dandy blender, soup is minutes away.

*Greengrocers pose at the Baltimore Farmers' Market, c.1930.*

Baltimore Museum of Industry

# POTATO SOUP

6 medium potatoes, peeled and cubed
1 large onion, sliced
⅓ cup diced green pepper
1 ham hock
3 cups water
1½ cups milk
½ cup half-and-half
1 teaspoon celery salt
1 teaspoon salt
Dash of pepper
Dash of red pepper
3 tablespoons butter or margarine, softened
Paprika
Fresh parsley sprigs (optional)

Combine potatoes, onion, green pepper, ham hock, and water in a 3-quart Dutch oven; bring to a boil. Reduce heat; cover and simmer 25 minutes or until potatoes are tender. Remove and discard ham hock. Drain vegetables, reserving ½ cup cooking liquid.

Place vegetables and reserved cooking liquid in container of an electric blender; process until smooth. Combine pureed vegetable mixture and next 7 ingredients in a medium saucepan, mixing well. Cook, stirring constantly, until soup is thoroughly heated. (Do not boil.)

Ladle soup into individual serving bowls. Sprinkle each serving with paprika, and garnish with fresh parsley sprigs, if desired. Yield: 2 quarts.

# CREAMY HERB POTATO SOUP

3 medium leeks
1 cup chopped celery
¾ cup chopped onion
3 tablespoons butter or margarine
4 cups peeled and diced potatoes
2 quarts chicken broth
1 teaspoon dried whole rosemary
2 teaspoons salt
2 cups whipping cream
3 tablespoons chopped fresh parsley

Remove and discard roots, tough outer leaves, and tops from leeks; wash leeks thoroughly, and coarsely chop.

Sauté leeks, celery, and onion in butter in a large Dutch oven 10 minutes or until tender. Stir in potatoes, chicken broth, rosemary, and salt; cover and bring to a boil. Reduce heat to low, and cook 20 minutes.

Stir in whipping cream, and heat to serving temperature. (Do not boil.) Serve hot in individual soup bowls, and garnish with chopped parsley. Yield: about 3 quarts.

*Ad for New Early Sunrise Potato seed, c.1890. Mr. Potato seems to be on the run from a soup kettle.*

# VICHYSSOISE

4 medium leeks
1 small onion, chopped
¼ cup butter or margarine
1 quart chicken broth
1 pound potatoes (about 4 medium), peeled and thinly sliced
1 teaspoon salt
2 cups milk
2 cups half-and-half
½ cup whipping cream
½ cup commercial sour cream
Chopped chives (optional)

Remove and discard roots, tough outer leaves, and tops from leeks; wash thoroughly, and thinly slice.

Sauté leeks and onion in butter in a large saucepan; add chicken broth, potatoes, and salt. Cook, uncovered, over medium heat 20 minutes or until potatoes are tender. Process 2 cups potato mixture in container of an electric blender until smooth; repeat procedure with remaining potato mixture.

Pour pureed potato mixture into a large bowl; add milk, half-and-half, whipping cream, and sour cream, stirring with a wire whisk until well blended and smooth. Cool mixture to room temperature; cover and chill thoroughly.

Serve Vichyssoise in chilled soup bowls; garnish with chives, if desired. Yield: about 2½ quarts.

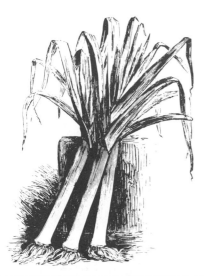

# BAKED-IN-A-PUMPKIN SOUP

1½ cups French bread
   crumbs
1 (6-inch diameter) pumpkin
   with 2-inch stem
⅔ cup finely chopped onion
¼ cup butter or margarine
½ teaspoon rubbed sage
¼ teaspoon salt
⅛ teaspoon pepper
⅛ teaspoon ground nutmeg
½ cup (2 ounces) shredded
   Swiss cheese
2 to 2½ cups chicken broth
1 bay leaf
½ cup whipping cream
Chopped fresh parsley
   (optional)

Spread bread crumbs in a shallow roasting pan. Bake at 300° for 15 minutes, stirring occasionally. Remove and set aside.

Cut a thin slice from bottom of pumpkin so that it will sit flat. Cut a 4-inch diameter crown or lid in top of pumpkin; remove and set lid aside. Remove and discard seeds and strings from pumpkin; set pumpkin aside.

Sauté onion in butter in a large skillet until tender. Add bread crumbs; cook 2 minutes, stirring constantly. Stir in sage, salt, pepper, and nutmeg. Remove from heat; stir in cheese. Spoon into pumpkin. Pour in enough chicken broth to fill within 1 inch of top of pumpkin. Top with bay leaf. Replace pumpkin lid.

Place pumpkin in an 8-inch square baking pan. Place on bottom rack of oven. Bake at 400° for 1½ hours. Remove and discard bay leaf. Gradually stir whipping cream into soup; garnish with parsley, if desired.

Ladle soup from pumpkin into individual bowls; serve immediately. Yield: about 1 quart.

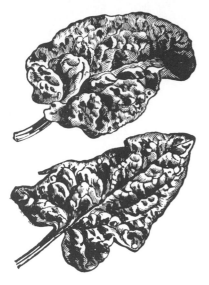

## SPINACH SOUP

1 cup finely chopped onion
2 tablespoons butter or
  margarine
2 tablespoons all-purpose
  flour
2 pounds fresh spinach,
  cleaned
1 quart chicken broth, divided
1 cup whipping cream
½ teaspoon salt
⅛ teaspoon grated whole
  nutmeg
Dash of red pepper
Paprika (optional)

Sauté onion in butter in a large Dutch oven until tender; add flour, stirring until smooth. Cook, stirring constantly, 4 minutes or until mixture is browned. Stir in spinach; simmer 10 minutes or until tender.

Place spinach mixture and 1 cup chicken broth in container of an electric blender; process until smooth. Return spinach mixture to Dutch oven. Stir in remaining chicken broth, whipping cream, salt, nutmeg, and pepper. Heat thoroughly. (Do not boil.) Serve warm in individual soup bowls; sprinkle with paprika, if desired. Yield: 2 quarts.

*Baked-in-a-Pumpkin Soup. Of those who taste it, someone will ask, "Where's the pumpkin?"*

## SALSIFY BISQUE

1½ cups scraped and sliced
  salsify
2 tablespoons chopped celery
½ teaspoon grated onion
½ teaspoon salt
Dash of red pepper
1½ to 1¾ cups half-and-half
1 egg yolk, beaten
Chopped fresh parsley

Combine salsify and a small amount of water in a small saucepan. Bring to a boil. Reduce heat; cover and simmer 10 minutes or until tender. Drain salsify well.

Place salsify, celery, onion, salt, pepper, and half-and-half in container of an electric blender; process until smooth. Transfer salsify mixture to top of a double boiler. Place over simmering water. Cook, stirring constantly, until thoroughly heated.

Gradually stir one-fourth of hot mixture into yolk; add to remaining hot mixture, stirring constantly. Cook over simmering water 2 minutes, stirring constantly.

Spoon soup into individual serving bowls; garnish with parsley. Serve immediately. Yield: 2½ cups.

*A squash seed packet, product of the Huth Seed Co. Inc., San Antonio.*

## COLD CURRIED SQUASH SOUP

2½ pounds yellow squash,
  thinly sliced
1 medium onion, thinly
  sliced
1 (10¾-ounce) can chicken
  broth, undiluted
1 tablespoon lemon juice
2 teaspoons curry powder
1 teaspoon salt
Dash of pepper
2 cups half-and-half
Chopped chives

Combine squash, onion, and chicken broth in a large Dutch oven; bring to a boil. Reduce heat; cover and simmer 15 minutes or until vegetables are tender. Stir in lemon juice, curry powder, salt, and pepper.

Spoon half of squash mixture into container of an electric blender, and process until smooth. Repeat with remaining squash mixture.

Place squash mixture in a large bowl; add half-and-half, stirring well. Cover and chill thoroughly. Spoon soup into chilled serving bowls; garnish with chives. Yield: 2 quarts.

*Three Sisters Brand tomatoes, early twentieth-century label.*

## CREAM OF TOMATO SOUP

1 (28-ounce) can whole
    tomatoes, undrained
1 thick slice onion
¾ teaspoon baking soda
½ teaspoon sugar
½ teaspoon salt
¼ teaspoon pepper
¼ cup butter or
    margarine
¼ cup all-purpose flour
1 quart milk, scalded

Combine first 6 ingredients in a large saucepan; boil 15 to 20 minutes. Strain tomato mixture through a sieve, mashing vegetables with back of a spoon; discard pulp. Return strained tomato mixture to saucepan, and set aside.

Melt butter in a medium saucepan over low heat; add flour, stirring until mixture is smooth. Cook 1 minute, stirring constantly. Gradually add 1 quart scalded milk; cook over medium heat, stirring constantly, until the mixture is slightly thickened.

Gradually stir milk mixture into reserved tomato mixture. Heat thoroughly. (Do not boil.) Spoon into individual serving bowls. Serve immediately. Yield: 1½ quarts.

## TOMATO BISQUE

2 pounds tomatoes, peeled
    and quartered
½ teaspoon baking soda
1 quart milk, scalded
¼ cup butter or margarine
1 teaspoon salt
¼ teaspoon pepper
½ cup finely crushed cracker
    crumbs (optional)

Place tomatoes in a small Dutch oven; cook, uncovered, over medium heat until tender. Add soda, stirring well. Strain tomato mixture through a fine-meshed sieve, mashing pulp with back of a spoon; discard the pulp.

Return strained tomato mixture to Dutch oven; add milk, butter, salt, pepper, and cracker crumbs, if desired. Cook over medium heat, stirring occasionally, until thoroughly heated.

Ladle into individual serving bowls. Serve warm. Yield: about 2 quarts.

## TURNIP SOUP

3 pounds meaty lamb neck
   bones
3 large onions, sliced
3 large bunches celery,
   cleaned and cut into 1-inch
   slices
4½ quarts water, divided
1 teaspoon salt
½ teaspoon pepper
5 large turnips, peeled and
   sliced
½ cup whipping cream

Combine neck bones, onion, celery, 3½ quarts water, salt, and pepper in a large Dutch oven. Bring to a boil. Reduce heat; cook, uncovered, 4½ hours. Remove from heat; strain broth through several layers of damp cheesecloth, discarding bones and vegetables. Chill broth overnight. Remove and discard fat. Set broth aside.

Place turnips and remaining water in a large saucepan; bring to a boil. Cook 25 minutes or until tender; drain. Process turnips through a food mill or sieve, reserving liquid from turnips; discard pulp.

Combine turnip liquid and lamb broth in Dutch oven; bring to a boil. Reduce heat; simmer, uncovered, 10 minutes. Gradually stir in whipping cream; heat thoroughly. Serve immediately in individual soup bowls. Yield: about 2 quarts.

## WATERCRESS SOUP

⅓ cup finely chopped onion
3 tablespoons butter or
   margarine
4 cups chopped fresh
   watercress leaves and stems
½ teaspoon salt
3 tablespoons all-purpose
   flour
1½ quarts chicken broth
2 egg yolks, lightly beaten
½ cup whipping cream

Sauté onion in butter in a small Dutch oven over medium heat 5 minutes or until tender. Stir in watercress and salt; cover and cook 5 minutes or until leaves are wilted and tender. Sprinkle flour over watercress; cook 3 minutes, stirring constantly. Stir in chicken broth; simmer 5 minutes.

Place 1 to 2 cups of watercress mixture in container of an electric blender; process until smooth. Transfer pureed mixture to a large saucepan. Repeat procedure with remaining watercress mixture.

Combine egg yolks and whipping cream in a small mixing bowl, mixing well; gradually add 1 cup pureed watercress mixture, stirring constantly. Gradually pour yolk mixture into remaining pureed watercress mixture, stirring well; cook over low heat 2 minutes or until thoroughly heated.

Ladle soup into individual serving bowls. Soup may be served warm or chilled. Yield: 1½ quarts.

*Three kinds of turnips, from Peter Henderson & Co. catalogue, 1891.*

## VEGETABLE SOUP PUREE

2 cups peeled, diced potatoes
1 cup chopped onion
1 cup green peas
1 cup chopped green beans
1 cup sliced carrots
1 cup lima beans
½ cup sliced celery
2 cups chicken broth
1 quart milk
1 teaspoon salt
Fresh parsley sprigs (optional)

Combine first 8 ingredients in a small Dutch oven; bring to a boil. Reduce heat; cover and simmer 20 minutes. Remove from heat, and cool slightly.

Puree mixture in a food mill or blender, discarding any vegetable hulls. Return vegetable puree to Dutch oven. Gradually add milk, beating well with a wire whisk. Stir in salt. Place over medium heat, and cook until thoroughly heated. (Do not boil.) Ladle into warm soup bowls, and serve immediately. Garnish each serving with parsley, if desired. Yield: about 2 quarts.

## CREAM OF VEGETABLE SOUP

1 quart water
1 cup chopped fresh green beans
1 cup chopped fresh asparagus
1 cup fresh lima beans
1 cup whole kernel corn
1 teaspoon salt
3 tablespoons butter or margarine
3 tablespoons all-purpose flour
3 cups milk
½ teaspoon pepper

Combine first 6 ingredients in a large Dutch oven; bring to a boil. Reduce heat; cover and simmer 20 minutes or until vegetables are tender. Drain. Reserve vegetables and 2 cups cooking liquid; set aside.

Melt butter in a large Dutch oven over low heat; add flour, stirring until smooth. Cook 1 minute, stirring constantly. Gradually add milk; cook over medium heat, stirring constantly, until thickened and bubbly. Stir in pepper. Gradually stir in reserved vegetables and cooking liquid. Continue to cook over medium heat until thoroughly heated.

Ladle soup into individual soup bowls, and serve immediately. Yield: about 2 quarts.

*A picture from a seed catalogue shows a satisfied customer reveling in a bumper crop of every possible kind of vegetable.*

*Food mill is excellent for pureeing soup vegetables.*

## CREAM OF ZUCCHINI SOUP

¼ cup butter or margarine
2 pounds zucchini, unpeeled and thinly sliced
¼ cup finely chopped shallot
2 cloves garlic, finely chopped
3¼ cups chicken broth, divided
1 cup whipping cream
½ teaspoon salt
¼ teaspoon curry powder
Seasoned croutons

Melt butter in a small Dutch oven over low heat. Add zucchini, shallot, and garlic; cover and cook 15 minutes, stirring occasionally.

Place mixture in container of an electric blender; add 1 cup chicken broth. Process until smooth. Pour mixture into Dutch oven; add remaining broth, whipping cream, salt, and curry powder. Cook over medium heat, stirring frequently, until hot.

Ladle soup into individual serving bowls; garnish with croutons, and serve warm. Soup may also be served chilled. Yield: about 1½ quarts.

The trio of recipes on this page will serve to settle our minds upon the difference between purees and cream soups. Note that in Vegetable Soup Puree, the vegetables themselves make up the body of the mixture; no cream or thickener is needed. But Cream of Zucchini contains heavy cream, while Cream of Vegetable Soup gets a creamy consistency from milk that is thickened by a butter-flour roux. From these examples, it will be simple for the cook to improvise other soups, utilizing those vegetables that are most preferred and most plentiful at the moment.

# ONE-DISH MEALS

How does soup become a meal in itself? Just think of meat, poultry, seafood, and all the high-protein legumes; with skill, any of these may be turned into well-balanced meals. We pile in vegetables, pasta, meatballs, and seasonings with a generous hand and serve it up with good bread and butter on the side. "Four hours before you goe to dinner or supper, hang over ye fire a good pot of water, with a pritty piece of beef and let it boyle an houre. Yn put in a marrow bone or 2 & let it boyle an houre longer. . . . " This was the beginning of the French Pottage recipe in an English cookbook used by Martha Washington for many years. It is so basic that it could be the beginning of Pot-au-Feu, the first recipe in this chapter.

The English had taken the French *potage*, added another *t*, and moved the accent to the first syllable. The antique recipe used a liaison of egg yolks for a sumptuous finish.

Seafood chowders developed in the coastal colonies as another way to use the gifts of the sea. Fish chowders were popular all the way down to Florida, clam and cod chowders evolving farther north. Fresh water trout became chowder for inlanders. Made with milk, these deluxe dishes may be thickened with flour or potatoes.

Every nationality has whole meal soups; this chapter borrows flavors from many ethnic cuisines, all now comfortably "Southern." Pepper Pot Soup was created by a cook in the Colonial Army at Valley Forge. Hunger was causing many desertions; General Washington appealed to his Pennsylvania Dutch cook. The depleted larder contained tripe, peppercorns, and a few scraps. With determination and skill, the cook turned the unlikely ingredients into nourishing soup — and a bit of history. A Mexican meal-in-a-bowl contains tortillas and meatballs; a German beef soup is full of homemade noodles.

There is no greater economy in nutrition than a hearty soup of beans or legumes, eaten with grains such as rice or cornbread. Such a meal is pure comfort in cold weather. For summertime, though, thoughts turn to cool, refreshing Gazpacho, a legacy from Spain.

*Minestrone, a traditional Italian soup, contains barley and pasta; vegetables may vary according to taste. It is but one of the full-meal soups in this collection; only salad, bread, and possibly dessert are needed.*

# MEAT AND POULTRY PLUS . . .

Preparing for Market,
*lithograph by Nathaniel
Currier, 1856.*

## POT-AU-FEU

3 pounds beef short
  ribs
3 quarts water
1 tablespoon salt
1 large onion, chopped
2 cups chopped leeks
1 cup diced turnips
⅔ cup chopped carrot
¼ cup chopped celery
¼ cup chopped
  parsnips
3 whole cloves
1 clove garlic, minced
1 tablespoon butter or
  margarine

Combine first 3 ingredients in
a large stockpot; bring to a boil.
Skim surface frequently with a
flat ladle to remove grayish
scum. Reduce heat; cover and
simmer 4 hours. Remove from
heat, and set aside to cool.

Remove short ribs from stock;
set stock aside. Remove meat
from ribs; discard bones. Chop
meat; cover and refrigerate.

Line a sieve with several layers
of damp cheesecloth. Strain
stock through cheesecloth into
a bowl. Cover and refrigerate
overnight. Carefully lift solidified fat from top of stock; discard fat.

Return stock and meat to
stockpot; add remaining ingredients. Bring to a boil. Reduce
heat; cover and simmer 1 hour
or until vegetables are tender.
Remove and discard cloves.
Spoon soup into individual
soup bowls; serve immediately.
Yield: 2 quarts.

## PEPPER POT

2 quarts beef broth
1 (24-ounce) can tripe,
  drained and coarsely
  chopped
2 cups peeled, diced potatoes
¾ cup chopped onion
¾ cup thinly sliced celery
½ cup chopped green pepper
½ teaspoon dried whole
  thyme
¼ teaspoon salt
¼ teaspoon pepper
¼ teaspoon marjoram leaves
Dash of ground allspice

Combine all ingredients in a
large Dutch oven; bring to a
boil. Reduce heat; cover and
simmer 2 hours or until tripe is
tender. Serve immediately in individual soup bowls. Yield: 3
quarts.

# MEXICAN MEATBALL SOUP

Just reading the ingredient list is enough to whet appetites for Mexican Meatball Soup. From cut-up flour tortillas to cumin and fresh cilantro, it is South-of-the-Border in flavor, but not to be confused with chili. To make a meal of it, add salad and hot, buttered tortillas. Fresh cilantro, the leaf of the coriander plant, may be hard to find. Substitute 2 to 3 teaspoons (or to taste) dried cilantro.

*Maize for tortillas is being ground on a metate in this 1800s engraving.*

1 pound ground chuck
3 flour tortillas, cut into 1- x ⅛-inch strips
1 egg, lightly beaten
½ teaspoon salt
½ teaspoon ground cumin, divided
¼ teaspoon pepper
1 clove garlic, minced
2 tablespoons vegetable oil
1 medium onion, chopped
1 quart water
1 (16-ounce) can whole tomatoes, undrained and chopped
1 (4-ounce) can chopped green chiles
¼ cup chopped fresh cilantro
3 beef-flavored bouillon cubes

Combine meat, tortilla strips, egg, salt, ¼ teaspoon cumin, pepper, and garlic in a medium mixing bowl; mix well. Shape mixture into 1-inch balls.

Brown meatballs in oil in a medium Dutch oven over medium heat; set aside, reserving drippings in Dutch oven.

Sauté onion in drippings until tender; drain off drippings and discard. Add water, tomatoes, green chiles, cilantro, bouillon cubes, and remaining cumin to Dutch oven. Cook, uncovered, over medium heat 30 minutes, stirring frequently. Return meatballs to Dutch oven, and cook an additional 15 minutes over medium heat.

Serve immediately in warm soup bowls. Yield: 1½ quarts.

## FILLED NOODLE SOUP

2 pounds beef stew meat, cut into 1-inch cubes
2 quarts water
1 (16-ounce) can whole tomatoes, undrained and chopped
1 medium onion, diced
1 tablespoon salt
¾ teaspoon pepper
1 medium cabbage, shredded
6 carrots, scraped and sliced
5 stalks celery, sliced
½ cup uncooked regular rice
2 small red peppers (optional)
1 pound ground beef
1 small onion, chopped
4 eggs, lightly beaten
2 cups all-purpose flour
1 teaspoon baking powder

Combine stew meat and water in a large stockpot; bring to a boil. Add tomatoes, diced onion, salt, and pepper. Reduce heat; cover and simmer 2 hours, stirring occasionally. Add cabbage, carrots, celery, rice, and red peppers, if desired; simmer, uncovered, 1 hour, stirring frequently.

Cook ground beef in a skillet over medium heat until browned, stirring to crumble; remove meat with a slotted spoon, reserving drippings in skillet. Sauté chopped onion in drippings until tender; drain well. Combine cooked ground beef and sautéed onion in a small mixing bowl, stirring well; set aside.

Place eggs in a medium mixing bowl; gradually add flour and baking powder, stirring until mixture forms a soft dough. Turn dough out onto a floured surface, and knead 2 minutes.

Divide dough in half. Roll each half to 1/16-inch thickness on a lightly floured surface; cut each into a 16- x 12-inch rectangle. Cut each rectangle into twelve 4-inch squares. Let dough rest on floured surface at room temperature 30 minutes.

Place a heaping tablespoon of ground beef mixture in center of each square. Moisten edges

## GERMAN BEEF-NOODLE SOUP

1 (3-pound) boneless chuck roast
1 medium onion, sliced
1 tablespoon vegetable oil
2 quarts water
2 teaspoons salt
½ teaspoon pepper
4 medium tomatoes, peeled and chopped
Homemade Noodles (page 13)

Brown roast and onion in oil in a large Dutch oven until meat is browned on all sides. Add water, salt, and pepper. Bring to a boil. Reduce heat; cover and simmer 3½ hours. Cut roast into bite-size pieces. Stir in tomatoes and half the Homemade Noodles (reserve remaining noodles for use in other recipes). Cover and simmer 30 minutes or until noodles are tender. Spoon into individual serving bowls. Serve immediately. Yield: 3 quarts.

## BEEF-VERMICELLI SOUP

2½ gallons water
1 (6-pound) beef rump roast, cut into ½-inch cubes
2 tablespoons salt
½ teaspoon pepper
4 large turnips, peeled and cubed
1 pound carrots, scraped and sliced
1 (12-ounce) package vermicelli, broken into ½-inch pieces

Combine water, beef, and salt in a large stockpot; bring to a boil. Reduce heat; cook, uncovered, 1 hour, skimming surface frequently with a flat ladle to remove grayish scum. Stir in pepper, turnips, and carrots; continue to cook, uncovered, 1½ hours, stirring occasionally.

Stir in vermicelli; cook, uncovered, 30 minutes. Ladle into individual soup bowls; serve warm. Yield: 2 gallons.

with water; fold squares in half. Press pastry edges firmly together with a fork.

Gently stir filled noodles into soup; cover and simmer an additional 30 minutes. Ladle into individual soup bowls, and serve immediately. Yield: 5 quarts.

Left: *Filled Noodle Soup simmers away over the fire in the restored kitchen at the Terrill Home in Fredericksburg, Texas.* Above: *Additional noodles are in the process of being filled before adding them to the soup.*

*Lamb and Vegetable Soup, great with French bread.*

## MACARONI-BEEF SOUP

2 quarts beef broth
1½ cups diced cooked beef
¾ cup shelled fresh lima
   beans
¼ pound fresh green beans,
   cut into ½-inch pieces
½ cup peeled, diced
   potatoes
½ cup diced carrots
½ cup diced celery
½ cup diced onion
½ cup diced cabbage
2 cloves garlic, minced
1 teaspoon chopped fresh
   thyme
½ cup elbow macaroni

Combine all ingredients, except macaroni, in a large Dutch oven; bring to a boil. Reduce heat; cover and simmer until vegetables are tender.

Return to a boil. Stir in macaroni; simmer 15 minutes or until macaroni is tender. Ladle into individual soup bowls; serve warm. Yield: 3 quarts.

## LAMB AND VEGETABLE SOUP

1 (6- to 7-pound) leg of lamb
1 gallon water
1 cup finely chopped carrots
1 cup finely chopped potatoes
1 cup finely chopped onion
1 cup finely chopped tomato
1 cup finely shredded cabbage
1 cup finely chopped turnips
1 teaspoon salt
½ teaspoon pepper

Place lamb and water in a large stockpot; bring to a boil. Reduce heat; cover and simmer 3 hours. Remove from heat; let cool. Cover and refrigerate overnight. Skim off fat, and discard.

Remove lamb, reserving broth in stockpot. Cut meat from bone, and cut into bite-size pieces; discard bone. Return meat to broth. Add remaining ingredients, stirring well.

Bring to a boil. Reduce heat; cover and simmer 3 hours. Serve hot in individual soup bowls. Yield: 1 gallon.

**M**acaroni-Beef Soup utilizes cooked meat, so it is a prime recipe for the creative recycling of roast beef, and such is the stuff of everyday life. But there are some times when we must be prepared to spend good money for a fine main-dish soup. Lamb and Vegetable Soup is a case in point: In the guise of soup, a lamb leg will serve twice as many people as will the same leg when roasted. And that is a consideration to be taken seriously!

## HAM BONE SOUP

1 (2-pound) meaty ham bone
¼ teaspoon pepper
3 medium onions, finely
  chopped
3 quarts water
4 medium potatoes, peeled
  and cubed
1 small cabbage, cleaned and
  shredded
1 (28-ounce) can whole
  tomatoes, undrained
Dash of red pepper
Salt to taste

Combine ham bone, pepper, onion, and water in a large stockpot; bring to a boil. Reduce heat; cover and simmer 3 hours.

Add potatoes, cabbage, tomatoes, and red pepper; simmer an additional hour. Remove ham bone from soup; remove meat from bone and chop, discarding bone. Add chopped meat to soup; skim off and discard excess fat from soup. Stir in salt.

Ladle soup into individual serving bowls; serve warm. Yield: 5½ quarts.

*Note*: A cooked ham bone with ham scraps may be used. If cooked ham is used, reduce initial cooking time to 2 hours.

*"The Mart," Monticello Avenue, Norfolk, Virginia, 1913.*

## GOLDEN CHICKEN SOUP

1 (5-pound) stewing hen,
  cut up
2 medium onions, thinly
  sliced
1 tablespoon salt
½ teaspoon pepper
1 gallon water
1 pound carrots, scraped and
  cut into 1-inch pieces
1 pound parsnips, cleaned
  and cut into 1-inch pieces
5 stalks celery, cleaned and
  cut into 1-inch pieces
1 large bunch fresh parsley

Combine chicken, onion, salt, pepper, and water in a large Dutch oven; bring to a boil. Reduce heat; cover and simmer 20 minutes.

Add carrots, parsnips, and celery; stir well. Place parsley on top of soup; cover and simmer an additional 3 hours.

Remove chicken and vegetables from soup; set aside. Discard parsley. Strain broth through several layers of damp cheesecloth. Remove chicken from bones, and coarsely chop; return chicken and vegetables to strained broth. Place over medium heat, and cook until thoroughly heated.

Ladle soup into individual serving bowls; serve warm. Yield: about 1 gallon.

## CHICKEN VEGETABLE SOUP

2 quarts chicken bouillon
1 cup sliced carrots
1 cup fresh or frozen green
  peas
1 cup chopped celery
1 teaspoon salt
2 cups diced cooked chicken
½ (8-ounce) package
  medium-size egg noodles,
  cooked and drained
1 teaspoon dried whole
  rosemary
1 teaspoon dried whole thyme

Combine first 5 ingredients in a large Dutch oven; bring to a boil. Stir in remaining ingredients. Reduce heat; cover and simmer 15 minutes or until vegetables are tender. Ladle into individual soup bowls; serve warm. Yield: about 3 quarts.

*Ladies' luncheon featured soup at Margaret Springfield's, Waynesville, North Carolina, 1900.*

## CHICKEN AND CORN SOUP

1 (3½-pound) broiler-fryer,
   cut up
2 quarts water
1 medium onion, chopped
¼ cup chopped fresh parsley
1 teaspoon salt
1 teaspoon pepper
2 bay leaves
6 ears fresh yellow corn,
   cleaned and kernels cut
   from cob
1 cup uncooked egg noodles
Chopped hard-cooked egg

Combine chicken, water, onion, parsley, salt, pepper, and bay leaves in a large Dutch oven; bring to a boil. Reduce heat; cover and simmer 45 minutes or until chicken is tender. Remove chicken from broth; cool. Bone chicken, and cut meat into bite-size pieces; set aside.

Add corn to chicken broth; simmer, uncovered, 20 minutes, stirring frequently. Stir in noodles, and simmer an additional 10 minutes, stirring frequently. Remove and discard bay leaves. Stir in chicken, and cook until thoroughly heated.

Serve soup immediately in warm soup bowls; garnish each serving with chopped hard-cooked egg. Yield: 2 quarts.

## CHICKEN MULLIGATAWNY

1 large onion, sliced
1 medium-size green pepper,
   seeded and chopped
½ cup chopped carrots
½ cup chopped celery
¼ cup butter or margarine
¼ cup all-purpose flour
5 cups rich chicken stock
2 cups chopped cooked
   chicken
2 tablespoons chopped fresh
   parsley
1 teaspoon curry powder
1 teaspoon salt
¼ teaspoon pepper
Hot cooked rice

Sauté onion, green pepper, carrots, and celery in butter in a medium Dutch oven until vegetables are tender. Stir in flour; cook over medium heat 5 minutes, stirring constantly. Gradually add next 6 ingredients, stirring constantly; bring to a boil. Reduce heat; cover and simmer 1 hour. Serve over hot cooked rice in individual bowls. Yield: 2 quarts.

## CHICKEN NOODLE SOUP

1 (5-pound) stewing hen,
  cut up
1 medium onion, quartered
2 stalks celery, cleaned and
  cut into 2-inch pieces
1 carrot, cut into 2-inch
  pieces
1 cup chopped fresh
  parsley
1 tablespoon salt
1 teaspoon whole allspice
3 quarts water
Homemade Noodles (page 13)

Combine all ingredients, except Homemade Noodles, in a large stockpot; bring to a boil. Skim surface frequently with a flat ladle to remove grayish scum. Reduce heat; simmer, uncovered, 2 hours, stirring occasionally. Remove from heat, and cool. Remove chicken; cool. Bone chicken, and coarsely chop meat. Set chicken aside.

Strain stock through several layers of damp cheesecloth; discard vegetables and spices. Skim off any excess fat, and return stock to stockpot.

Bring stock to a boil; stir in Homemade Noodles. Cover and cook 30 minutes or until noodles are tender. Stir in reserved chicken, and heat thoroughly. Ladle soup into warm serving bowls, and serve immediately. Yield: about 1 gallon.

## TOMATO-VERMICELLI SOUP

1 (14½-ounce) can whole
  tomatoes, undrained
2 quarts chicken broth
½ (8-ounce) package
  vermicelli, broken into
  ½-inch pieces
2 cups diced cooked chicken
Salt and pepper to taste
Chopped fresh parsley
Grated Parmesan cheese

Press tomatoes through a sieve, using the back of a spoon; discard pulp. Combine tomato juice and chicken broth in a small Dutch oven; bring to a boil. Reduce heat; cover and simmer 30 minutes.

Return to a boil; add vermicelli. Reduce heat; cover and simmer 15 minutes. Stir in chicken and salt and pepper; heat thoroughly. Ladle into individual soup bowls; sprinkle with parsley and Parmesan cheese. Serve warm. Yield: about 2 quarts.

*Tomato-Vermicelli Soup, rich with chicken, to serve with Parmesan cheese.*

# CHICKEN SOUP AND FILLED DUMPLINGS

1 (3-pound) broiler-fryer,
  cut up
1 small onion, thinly sliced
2 stalks celery, cleaned and
  cut into 2-inch pieces
1 carrot, sliced
2 sprigs fresh parsley
1 bay leaf
2 teaspoons salt
¼ teaspoon pepper
1½ quarts water
Filled Dumplings
Chopped fresh parsley

Combine chicken, onion, celery, carrot, parsley sprigs, bay leaf, salt, pepper, and water in a large Dutch oven; bring to a boil. Reduce heat; cover and simmer 1 hour.

Remove chicken; set aside. Strain broth through several layers of damp cheesecloth. Reserve vegetables for other uses. Skim fat from broth. Return broth to Dutch oven.

Remove chicken from bones; chop meat, reserving 2 tablespoons chopped chicken for use in Filled Dumplings. Add chopped chicken to broth.

Bring broth to a boil. Reduce heat; add Filled Dumplings to broth. Cover and simmer 10 minutes.

Ladle soup and Filled Dumplings into individual serving bowls; garnish with chopped fresh parsley. Serve warm. Yield: about 2 quarts.

**Filled Dumplings:**

1 egg
1 tablespoon water
⅔ cup all-purpose flour
¼ teaspoon salt
2 tablespoons reserved
  chopped cooked chicken
2 tablespoons finely chopped
  cooked spinach
1 egg, lightly beaten
1 tablespoon fine, dry
  breadcrumbs
1½ teaspoons grated onion
Dash of salt
Dash of ground thyme
Dash of ground nutmeg

Combine 1 egg and water in a small mixing bowl; beat with a wire whisk. Add flour and ¼ teaspoon salt, stirring well.

Turn dough out onto a lightly floured surface, and knead 2 minutes. Cover and let rest 20 minutes.

Combine reserved chicken, spinach, lightly beaten egg, breadcrumbs, onion, salt, thyme, and nutmeg in a small mixing bowl; mix well.

Roll dough to 1/16-inch thickness on a lightly floured surface; cut with a 2-inch biscuit cutter. Place ½ teaspoon chicken mixture in center of half of the dumplings. Moisten edges, and cover with remaining dumplings; seal edges of each dumpling with tines of a fork. Yield: about 2 dozen.

## TORTILLA SOUP

1 (5-pound) stewing hen,
  cut up
3 quarts water
3 tomatoes, peeled and
  chopped
2 medium onions, chopped
1 green pepper, seeded and
  chopped
1 (16-ounce) can refried
  beans
1 lime, halved
1 green chile, chopped
2 large cloves garlic, minced
1 teaspoon chili powder
½ teaspoon red pepper
½ teaspoon pepper
1 teaspoon salt
Condiments

Combine chicken, water, tomatoes, onion, green pepper, beans, lime halves, green chile, garlic, chili powder, and pepper in a large stockpot; bring to a boil. Reduce heat; cover and simmer 2 hours. Remove chicken from broth; cool. Bone chicken and cut into bite-size pieces; return chicken to broth. Refrigerate broth overnight.

Skim off and discard fat that has risen to the surface. Discard lime halves, and stir in salt. Cook soup over medium heat until thoroughly heated. Serve immediately in warm bowls with the following condiments: chopped fresh cilantro, chopped tomatoes, chopped onion, lime slices, shredded Monterey Jack cheese, and fried corn tortillas. Yield: 5 quarts.

*Tortilla Soup, photographed in Mission, Texas, is a favorite dish of the area.*

*Prize Brown Leghorn chickens on trade card, c.1890.*

## RIO GRANDE TORTILLA SOUP

1½ quarts water
4 beef-flavored bouillon cubes
2 chicken-flavored bouillon cubes
10 corn tortillas, divided
1 medium onion, quartered and thinly sliced
2 cloves garlic, finely chopped
1 jalapeño pepper, seeded and finely chopped
½ cup plus 2 tablespoons vegetable oil, divided
½ cup tomato sauce
1 teaspoon salt
1 teaspoon ground cumin
1 teaspoon chili powder
1 teaspoon Worcestershire sauce
1 cup diced cooked chicken
2 tomatoes, peeled and chopped
2 cups (8 ounces) shredded Monterey Jack cheese
1 avocado, peeled, seeded, and diced
Chopped fresh cilantro leaves
Lime wedges (optional)
Hot sauce (optional)

Combine water, bouillon cubes, and 3 tortillas in a small Dutch oven; bring to a boil. Reduce heat; simmer, uncovered, 1 hour, stirring occasionally to break up tortillas.

Strain broth through a fine-meshed sieve, pressing tortillas through sieve using back of a wooden spoon. Add water to tortilla-broth mixture to equal 6 cups; set aside.

Add onion, garlic, jalapeño pepper, and 2 tablespoons oil to Dutch oven; sauté 3 minutes. Stir in reserved tortilla-broth mixture, tomato sauce, salt, cumin, chili powder, and Worcestershire sauce; bring to a boil. Reduce heat; cover and simmer 1 hour.

Add chicken and tomatoes to broth; simmer 10 minutes.

Cut remaining tortillas into 2- x ½-inch strips. Fry strips in remaining oil in a heavy skillet until crisp; drain well on paper towels.

Place several crisp tortilla strips in the bottom of each

*"Turkeys Almost Ready for Thanksgiving,"* 1890.

individual bowl; top with 2 tablespoons grated cheese and 1 tablespoon avocado. Ladle soup into each bowl; sprinkle with additional tortilla pieces and cheese. Garnish with cilantro leaves. Serve with lime wedges and hot sauce, if desired. Yield: about 1½ quarts.

## TURKEY-NOODLE SOUP

1 turkey carcass containing about 1½ pounds leftover turkey
1 large onion, finely chopped
2 teaspoons salt
½ teaspoon pepper
1 sprig fresh thyme
3 quarts water
Homemade Noodles (page 13)

Combine first 6 ingredients in a large stockpot; bring to a boil. Reduce heat; cover and simmer 2 hours or until meat falls off the bones.

Remove bones and meat from broth; discard bones. Coarsely chop meat; return to broth.

Bring broth to a boil; reduce heat. Drop noodles into simmering soup. Cook, uncovered, 10 minutes or until noodles are tender.

Ladle soup and noodles into individual serving bowls; serve warm. Yield: about 3 quarts.

## CREAMY TURKEY SOUP

1½ quarts turkey broth, divided
1 large onion, chopped
2 stalks celery, chopped
1 medium carrot, scraped and diced
½ cup butter or margarine
¾ cup all-purpose flour
1 cup warm half-and-half
½ teaspoon salt
Pinch of white pepper
½ cup diced cooked turkey
½ cup cooked regular rice

Combine ½ quart turkey broth, onion, celery, and carrot in a large saucepan; bring to a boil. Reduce heat; cover and simmer until vegetables are tender. Remove from heat; reserve vegetables and broth.

Melt butter in a small Dutch oven over low heat; add flour, stirring until smooth. Cook 1 minute, stirring constantly. Gradually add remaining 1 quart turkey broth; cook over medium heat, stirring constantly, until thickened and bubbly. Gradually stir in warm half-and-half, salt, and pepper. Add reserved vegetables and broth, turkey, and rice. Cook over medium heat until thoroughly heated. Ladle into individual soup bowls; serve warm. Yield: about 2¼ quarts.

# CHOWDERS FOR ANY OCCASION

*Florida Fish Chowder is a light version of traditional recipe using butter, not salt pork.*

## FLORIDA FISH CHOWDER

2 cups water
1 cup peeled, diced potatoes
1 cup sliced carrots
½ cup chopped celery
2½ teaspoons salt, divided
1 medium onion, thinly sliced
2 tablespoons butter or margarine
2 pounds red snapper fillets, cut into 1-inch pieces
1 teaspoon Worcestershire sauce
¼ teaspoon white pepper
2 cups milk
2 tablespoons all-purpose flour
Paprika

Combine water, potatoes, carrots, celery, and ½ teaspoon salt in a medium saucepan. Bring to a boil. Reduce heat; cover and simmer 15 minutes. Set aside.

Sauté onion in butter in a large Dutch oven until tender. Add fish and Worcestershire sauce; cook over medium heat 1 minute, stirring gently. Add cooked vegetables and liquid, remaining salt, and pepper. Cover and simmer 10 minutes.

Gradually stir milk into flour, blending until smooth. Stir milk mixture into fish mixture. Cook over low heat 15 minutes or until thoroughly heated. (Do not boil.) Spoon chowder into individual serving bowls; sprinkle with paprika. Yield: 2 quarts.

## TROUT CHOWDER

2½ cups sliced fresh okra
2 tablespoons vegetable oil
¾ cup finely diced onion
1 clove garlic
2 teaspoons coarsely ground
   black pepper
1 teaspoon salt
1 teaspoon dried whole basil
½ teaspoon ground turmeric
½ teaspoon paprika
½ teaspoon dried whole
   oregano
½ teaspoon dried whole
   rosemary
3 cups diced freshwater trout
   fillets
2 cups water
1 medium tomato, peeled and
   diced
1 (6-ounce) can tomato paste
3 tablespoons soy sauce
2 tablespoons Worcestershire
   sauce
2 large bay leaves

Sauté sliced okra in oil in a small Dutch oven 5 minutes. Add onion; sauté an additional 5 minutes or until tender. Stir in next 8 ingredients; cook 2 minutes over medium heat. Add fish; continue to cook over medium heat, stirring constantly, until fish flakes easily when tested with a fork. Stir in remaining ingredients; bring to a boil. Reduce heat to low; cover and simmer 20 minutes. Remove and discard bay leaves.

Ladle soup into individual bowls; serve warm. Yield: 2 quarts.

## COD CHOWDER

¼ pound salt pork, rinsed and
   cubed
1 large onion, thinly sliced
2 pounds cod fillets, cut into
   1-inch pieces
4 medium-size red potatoes,
   peeled and sliced
1 quart boiling water
2 cups milk
2 teaspoons salt
¼ teaspoon pepper
6 English muffins, split,
   buttered, and toasted

Cook salt pork in a large Dutch oven until browned and crisp; discard pork. Sauté onion in pork drippings until tender. Add fish, potatoes, and water. Bring to a boil. Reduce heat; cover and simmer 20 minutes. Gradually add milk, salt, and pepper, stirring constantly. Cook over medium heat 10 minutes or until thoroughly heated. (Do not boil.)

Place 1 English muffin half in each soup bowl. Spoon chowder over muffin. Serve immediately. Yield: about 2½ quarts.

*Fanciful label from a
can of Scarboro Beach
Clam Chowder, c.1890.*

## CLAM CHOWDER

2 large onions, thinly sliced
2 tablespoons butter or
   margarine
3 medium potatoes, peeled
   and cubed
1½ teaspoons salt
¼ teaspoon pepper
1 cup water
3 cups milk
1 cup (4 ounces) shredded
   Cheddar cheese
3 (6½-ounce) cans chopped,
   cooked clams, drained
Chopped fresh parsley

Sauté onion in butter in a large Dutch oven until tender; add potatoes, salt, pepper, and water. Bring to a boil. Reduce heat; cover and simmer 20 minutes or until potatoes are tender.

Combine milk and cheese in a small saucepan. Cook over low heat, stirring frequently, until cheese melts and mixture is well blended. Stir milk mixture and clams into potato mixture in Dutch oven. Continue to cook over medium heat until chowder is thoroughly heated.

Ladle into individual serving bowls, and garnish with parsley. Yield: 2½ quarts.

SCARBORO BEACH CLAM CHOWDER

*"Preparing the Chowder—Expectant Groups," by E. Champney, 1860.*

## MARION HARLAND'S CLAM CHOWDER

¼ pound salt pork, finely
    chopped
1 small onion, thinly
    sliced
6 small potatoes, peeled and
    thinly sliced
1 (16-ounce) can whole
    tomatoes, undrained
Dash of red pepper
1 quart cold water
6 whole allspice
6 whole cloves
4 Holland Rusk biscuits
½ cup milk
5 (6½-ounce) cans chopped
    cooked clams, undrained
Salt and pepper to taste

Cook salt pork in a large
Dutch oven over medium heat
until crisp. Remove salt pork

and discard; add onion to
drippings in Dutch oven, and
sauté until tender.

Add potatoes, tomatoes, red
pepper, and water. Place allspice
and cloves in a small cheesecloth bag. Tie securely, and
place spice bag in Dutch oven.
Bring to a boil. Reduce heat;
cover and simmer 1½ hours.

Soak biscuits in milk until all
liquid is absorbed; add toast
and clams to Dutch oven, stirring well to break up toast. Simmer an additional 15 minutes.

Remove spice bag and dis-
card; season chowder with salt
and pepper.

Ladle chowder into individual
serving bowls; serve warm.
Yield: about 2½ quarts.

*Marion Harland, 1860*

**Potato Peelers.**

# NEW ENGLAND CLAM CHOWDER

3 dozen soft-shell clams, shucked and undrained
2 ounces salt pork
1 medium onion, coarsely chopped
6 cups peeled, diced potatoes
2 bay leaves, crumbled
1 teaspoon salt
¼ teaspoon freshly ground black pepper
3 tablespoons butter or margarine
2 tablespoons all-purpose flour
1 quart milk, scalded
2 cups half-and-half, scalded

Drain clams, reserving liquid. Finely mince clams; set aside.

Sauté salt pork in a large Dutch oven until golden brown; remove salt pork and discard, reserving pan drippings in Dutch oven. Sauté onion in pan drippings until tender. Add potatoes, bay leaves, salt, and pepper; stir well. Add enough water to clam liquid to equal 3 cups; add to Dutch oven, stirring well. Bring to a boil. Reduce heat; cover and simmer 15 minutes.

Melt butter in a heavy saucepan over low heat; add flour, stirring until smooth. Cook 1 minute, stirring constantly. Gradually add scalded milk and half-and-half; cook over medium heat, stirring constantly, until slightly thickened.

Stir cream sauce and reserved minced clams into vegetable mixture; simmer 20 minutes. Serve warm in individual soup bowls. Yield: about 3½ quarts.

*Like your clam chowder red? Go for Manhattan-Style (front). For white, New England Clam Chowder.*

Culinary archaeology traces a forerunner of chowder back to the 1700s and the venerable Hannah Glasse. Her "Cheshire Pork-Pye for Sea," directed to mariners, was a layered affair of boiled and sliced salt pork and potatoes, seasoned, sluiced with water, and baked, covered. Sailors called it sea-pie. To this basic dish the settlers added sand-clams. As cooks became more inventive, they created their own versions of chowder, using whatever ingredients were on hand.

# MANHATTAN-STYLE CLAM CHOWDER

1 cup peeled, diced potatoes
1⅔ cups water
2 (14½-ounce) cans whole tomatoes, undrained and chopped
1 (10-ounce) package frozen cut green beans, thawed
1 cup chopped celery
⅔ cup chopped green pepper
¼ cup crumbled cooked bacon
1½ cups clam juice
2 tablespoons catsup
1 tablespoon Worcestershire sauce
1 tablespoon butter or margarine
1½ teaspoons Italian herbs
2 bay leaves
¼ teaspoon ground thyme
1 cup clams, drained and finely chopped

Combine potatoes and water in a small Dutch oven. Bring to a boil; boil 10 minutes. Add remaining ingredients except clams; stir well. Return to a boil. Reduce heat; cover and simmer 45 minutes. Add clams; cover and simmer 5 minutes. Remove and discard bay leaves.

Ladle into serving bowls. Serve warm. Yield: 3 quarts.

# STATEHOUSE OYSTER CHOWDER

4 slices bacon
2 cups water
1½ cups whole kernel corn, undrained
1 cup chopped celery
1 cup chopped carrots
1 cup peeled, diced potatoes
½ cup chopped onion
2 cups milk, divided
2 tablespoons cornstarch
½ cup chopped fresh parsley
2 tablespoons Worcestershire sauce
1½ teaspoons salt
¾ teaspoon dried whole oregano
¼ teaspoon pepper
3 (12-ounce) containers Standard oysters, drained

Cook bacon in a small Dutch oven until crisp; remove bacon, discarding drippings. Drain bacon on paper towels; crumble and set aside.

Place water, corn, celery, carrots, potatoes, onion, and reserved bacon in Dutch oven; bring to a boil. Cover and simmer 30 minutes.

Combine 1 cup milk and cornstarch in a small bowl, stirring well. Add cornstarch mixture, remaining milk, parsley, Worcestershire sauce, salt, oregano, and pepper to vegetables in Dutch oven; stir well. Bring to a boil; cook, uncovered, over high heat 1 minute, stirring constantly.

Stir in oysters; cover and simmer 15 minutes. Serve immediately in warm bowls. Yield: about 2 quarts.

The Island Queen *excursion steamer docked at Louisville, c.1890.*

## CHARLES BRONGER'S LOUISVILLE TURTLE SOUP

2 pounds turtle meat
1 teaspoon salt
¼ teaspoon pepper
1 gallon water
¼ cup all-purpose flour
3 large onions, quartered
2 medium potatoes, peeled and quartered
3 stalks celery, cleaned and cut into 3-inch pieces
2 carrots, scraped and cut into 2-inch pieces
½ cup fresh green beans
½ cup green peas
½ cup whole kernel corn
½ cup shredded cabbage
½ lemon, seeds removed
1 hard-cooked egg
1 (14½-ounce) can whole tomatoes, undrained
½ cup catsup
2 ounces tomato paste
½ cup claret or other dry red wine
1 teaspoon sugar
2 teaspoons whole allspice
¼ pod hot red pepper
Hard-cooked egg slices
Lemon slices

Combine turtle meat, salt, pepper, and water in a large stockpot; bring to a boil. Reduce heat; cover and simmer 2½ hours. Remove meat, and strain broth through several layers of damp cheesecloth; return broth to stockpot, and set meat aside.

Place flour in a small heavy skillet; cook over medium heat, stirring constantly, until flour browns. Gradually add browned flour to broth, stirring to blend well. Set aside.

Grind together reserved turtle meat, onions, potatoes, celery, carrots, green beans, peas, corn, cabbage, ½ lemon, and 1 hard-cooked egg into a large mixing bowl, using coarse blade of meat grinder. Add ground mixture with vegetable liquid to thickened broth in stockpot.

Press tomatoes through a fine-meshed sieve, using the back of a wooden spoon; add tomato pulp and liquid to stockpot. Stir in catsup, tomato paste, wine, and sugar.

Place whole allspice and red pepper in a small cheesecloth bag. Tie bag securely, and place in soup in stockpot.

Bring soup to a boil. Reduce heat; cover and simmer 1½ hours, stirring occasionally. Remove spice bag.

Ladle soup into individual serving bowls; garnish with egg and lemon slices. Serve warm. Yield: about 1½ gallons.

# FAVORITE VEGETABLE SOUPS

## BEAN SOUP

1½ cups dried pinto beans
9 cups water
1 (1-pound) meaty ham
   bone
½ cup finely chopped onion
1 teaspoon salt
½ teaspoon pepper

Combine beans and water in a large Dutch oven; bring to a boil. Remove from heat; cover and let stand 1 hour.

Add ham bone, onion, salt, and pepper to beans; bring to a boil. Reduce heat; cover and simmer 2 hours. Remove ham bone from soup; remove meat from bone, and return meat to soup. Discard bone.

Ladle soup into individual bowls, and serve immediately with hot cornbread. Yield: 1½ quarts.

## PINTO BEAN SOUP

½ cup chopped onion
1 clove garlic, minced
3 tablespoons butter or
   margarine
1 (16-ounce) can pinto
   beans, drained
1 (10¾-ounce) can chicken
   broth, diluted
½ teaspoon salt
¼ teaspoon pepper
½ cup tomato juice
Whipping cream

Sauté onion and garlic in butter in a medium Dutch oven; add beans, chicken broth, salt, and pepper. Simmer, uncovered, 10 minutes, stirring occasionally. Add tomato juice, and simmer until thoroughly heated.

Serve hot soup in individual mugs; add 1 tablespoon whipping cream to each mug. Serve immediately. Yield: 1 quart.

*Farm children picking green beans on a grand scale, perhaps for sale. Early twentieth century.*

## FRIJOLE-CHEESE SOUP

½ pound bacon, chopped
1 large onion, chopped
4 stalks celery, cleaned and
   chopped
1 (28-ounce) can whole
   tomatoes, undrained
1 cup water
4 cups (16 ounces) shredded
   Cheddar cheese
1 (16-ounce) can pinto beans,
   undrained and pureed
½ teaspoon red pepper
Pinch of ground cumin

Cook bacon in a small Dutch oven until crisp; remove bacon, reserving drippings in Dutch oven. Drain bacon on paper towels; set aside.

Sauté onion and celery in reserved drippings until tender. Drain off drippings, reserving vegetables in Dutch oven. Add tomatoes, reserved bacon, and water; stir well. Bring to a boil. Reduce heat; stir in cheese and pureed beans. Continue to cook over medium heat, uncovered, until cheese melts. Stir in red pepper and cumin.

Ladle soup into individual bowls; serve warm. Yield: about 1¼ quarts.

Brown Brothers

93

## SENATE NAVY BEAN SOUP

2 pounds dried navy beans
1 gallon water
1½ pounds smoked ham hocks
Salt to taste
½ teaspoon pepper
1 large onion, finely chopped
2 tablespoons butter or margarine

Combine beans and water in a large Dutch oven; bring to a boil. Remove from heat; cover and let stand 1 hour. Add ham hocks; bring to a boil. Reduce heat. Cover; simmer 3 hours. Remove meat from hamhocks. Chop meat; add to soup. Stir in salt and pepper.

Sauté onion in butter until browned. Stir into soup. Ladle soup into serving bowls; serve warm. Yield: about 5 quarts.

## BLACK BEAN SOUP

2 cups dried black beans
2 stalks celery, cleaned and chopped
½ cup chopped onion
¼ cup butter or margarine, divided
3½ quarts water
1 meaty ham bone
2 teaspoons salt
½ teaspoon pepper
¼ teaspoon dry mustard
3 tablespoons sherry
Lemon slices

Sort and wash beans; place in a large mixing bowl. Cover with water 2 inches above beans; let soak overnight. Drain well.

Sauté celery and onion in 2 tablespoons butter in a large Dutch oven until tender. Add water, ham bone, and beans; stir well. Bring to a boil. Reduce heat; cover and simmer 3 hours or until beans are tender. Remove and discard ham bone.

Drain bean mixture, reserving cooking liquid in Dutch oven. Puree beans, and return to Dutch oven; stir well. Bring to a boil; stir in remaining butter, salt, pepper, and mustard. Reduce heat; cover and simmer an additional 15 minutes. Stir in sherry.

Ladle soup into individual bowls; garnish each serving with a lemon slice. Serve warm. Yield: about 3 quarts.

*Senate Navy Bean Soup has been a tradition in the congressional dining rooms since the early 1900s. Below is a 1910 picture of one of the Senate dining rooms.*

U.S. Senate Curator's Office, Washington, D.C.

*Front to back: Red Bean, Senate Navy Bean, and Black Bean soups.*

GULF SALT SCHOONER

UNCOVERED SURFACE OF SALT DEPOSIT

BREAKING DOWN AN UNDER-CUT

FOOT OF MAIN SHAFT

*"The Salt Mine of Petite Anse" on Avery Island, by Charles Graham,* Harper's Weekly, *1883.*

## RED BEAN SOUP FROM AVERY ISLAND

Avery Island, Louisiana, of Tabasco sauce fame, has remained in the Marsh-Avery-McIlhenny families since 1818. Judge D.D. Avery, in 1861, became the owner, and in 1862, the entire island was discovered to be of salt. Because the Southern ports were blockaded, the salt works were used to supply the Confederate troops. The salt, which is of the purest quality, is still mined on the island.

1 small onion, chopped
½ cup chopped celery
2 cloves garlic, chopped
2 tablespoons butter or margarine
½ pound dried red kidney beans
2 bay leaves
2 sprigs fresh thyme
1 teaspoon Worcestershire sauce
¼ teaspoon Tabasco sauce
3 quarts water
½ pound cooked ground ham
½ teaspoon salt
¼ teaspoon pepper
Hard-cooked eggs, sieved
Lemon slices

Sauté chopped onion, celery, and garlic in butter in a large Dutch oven until tender. Add next 6 ingredients to Dutch oven; stir well. Bring mixture to a boil. Reduce heat; cover and simmer 3 hours.

Strain mixture through a sieve, pressing with the back of a spoon; discard excess pulp. Return soup to Dutch oven; stir in ham. Add salt and pepper, stirring well. Heat thoroughly. Remove and discard bay leaves.

Serve hot in individual bouillon cups. Garnish with sieved egg and a lemon slice. Yield: about 1½ quarts.

## BEAN AND BACON CHOWDER

1 cup dried navy beans
2 cups water
8 slices bacon
¾ cup chopped onion
¼ cup chopped green onion
½ cup chopped celery
1 clove garlic, minced
1 (28-ounce) can whole tomatoes, undrained
1 (10½-ounce) can beef broth, undiluted
½ cup hot water
⅓ cup tomato sauce
1 tablespoon sugar
1 teaspoon salt
¼ teaspoon pepper
½ teaspoon dried basil leaves

Combine beans and water in a 3-quart saucepan; bring to a boil. Reduce heat, and simmer 5 minutes. Remove from heat; cover and let stand 1 hour.

Cook bacon in a large skillet until crisp; drain on paper towels. Crumble and set aside, reserving 2 tablespoons drippings in skillet.

Sauté onion, celery, and garlic in reserved drippings until tender. Stir sautéed vegetables, reserved bacon, and remaining ingredients into beans. Bring to a boil. Reduce heat; cover and simmer 4½ hours or until beans are tender.

Spoon chowder into individual soup bowls; serve immediately. Yield: about 1½ quarts.

*Note:* Bean and Bacon Chowder may be made a day ahead and reheated to serve.

*Trade card for Magnolia Hams, c.1885. Today's advertisers would be loath to carry this message.*

# SPANISH BEAN SOUP

2 cups dried garbanzo beans
1 (½-pound) ham bone
2 quarts water
1 medium cabbage, finely shredded
1 whole pod red pepper
1 teaspoon salt
1 medium onion, sliced
2 tablespoons bacon drippings
1 teaspoon olive oil
¼ teaspoon garlic powder

Sort and wash beans; place in a large Dutch oven. Cover with water 2 inches above beans; let soak overnight. Drain well.

Place beans and ham bone in Dutch oven. Add 2 quarts water; bring to a boil. Reduce heat; cover and simmer 2 hours. Stir in cabbage, red pepper, and salt. Cover and simmer 1 hour. Remove ham bone; discard.

Sauté onion in drippings in a medium skillet until tender. Add to soup, stirring well. Combine olive oil and garlic powder in a small bowl. Stir into soup.

Serve soup hot in individual serving bowls. Yield: about 2½ quarts.

THAT WONDERFUL **MAGNOLIA HAM** PUT THIS HANDSOME BAY WINDOW ON ME.

97

*Lentil Soup: This legume goes back to Biblical days and is among the most nourishing foods we have.*

## LIMA BEAN CHOWDER

2 slices bacon
2 small onions, chopped
1 (16-ounce) can lima beans, drained
4 medium-size red potatoes, peeled and chopped
3 carrots, scraped and sliced
1½ teaspoons salt, divided
3½ cups boiling water
¼ cup butter or margarine
¼ cup all-purpose flour
2 cups milk
¼ teaspoon white pepper

Cook bacon in a large Dutch oven until crisp. Remove bacon, and drain on paper towels; reserve drippings in Dutch oven. Crumble bacon; set aside.

Sauté onion in reserved drippings until tender. Stir in crumbled bacon, lima beans, potatoes, carrots, and 1 teaspoon salt. Add boiling water, stirring well. Cover and simmer 1 hour.

Melt butter in a heavy saucepan over low heat; add flour, stirring until smooth. Cook 1 minute, stirring constantly. Gradually add milk; cook over medium heat, stirring constantly, until thickened and bubbly. Stir in remaining salt and pepper.

Add sauce to chowder, stirring well. Heat thoroughly. (Do not boil.) Serve hot in individual soup bowls. Yield: 2 quarts.

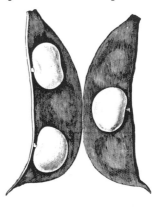

## LENTIL SOUP

3 quarts water
1 (1-pound) meaty soup bone
1 (28-ounce) can whole tomatoes, undrained and chopped
1 medium onion, chopped
1½ cups dried lentils
3 carrots, scraped and sliced
2 stalks celery, chopped
2 teaspoons salt
1 teaspoon pepper
10 frankfurters, cut into ¼-inch slices

Combine water and soup bone in a large stockpot; bring to a boil. Reduce heat; add tomatoes, onion, lentils, carrots, celery, salt, and pepper, stirring well. Simmer 1½ hours, stirring frequently. Remove from heat; remove and discard soup bone.

Stir in frankfurters; simmer an additional 30 minutes, stirring frequently. Serve immediately in warm soup bowls. Yield: 5½ quarts.

Americans are funny about beets. Like them or hate them, they are among the least utilized vegetables we grow. Not so in Europe in centuries past; not to like the trusty root would have meant having very little to eat. Borscht was originally made with a vegetable called the cow parsnip. To the soup was added fresh or fermented beet juice. Beets and cabbage were ever the dependable staples of the poor, so it is little wonder that so many variations arose. Our updated blender variation can be served warm or cold as a first course.

*Borscht: Poland, Russia, and the Balkans all had versions.*

## TRADITIONAL BORSCHT

2½ pounds cubed beef
1 (2-pound) soup bone
8 medium beets, peeled and cut into 2- x ⅛-inch strips
4 medium carrots, scraped and thinly sliced
6 stalks celery, thinly sliced
1 medium green pepper, seeded and finely chopped
1 small cabbage, chopped
2 medium onions, chopped
2 teaspoons salt
1 teaspoon pepper
1 (8-ounce) carton commercial sour cream

Combine beef and soup bone with water to cover in a large stockpot; bring to a boil. Reduce heat; cover and simmer 2 hours.

Add next 8 ingredients; bring to a boil. Reduce heat; cover and simmer 1½ hours. Remove and discard soup bone.

Ladle into individual soup bowls; garnish with a dollop of sour cream. Yield: about 2½ quarts.

## BORSCHT

1 medium onion, chopped
3 tablespoons bacon drippings
2 tablespoons butter or margarine
2 beef-flavored bouillon cubes
2 tablespoons sugar
1 cup boiling water
1 (16-ounce) can sliced beets, drained
Commercial sour cream

Sauté onion in bacon drippings and butter in a small skillet until tender. (Do not brown.) Dissolve bouillon cubes and sugar in boiling water. Combine sautéed onion, bouillon mixture, and beets in container of an electric blender; process 2 minutes or until smooth.

Transfer mixture to a heavy saucepan, and heat thoroughly. (Do not boil.) Ladle into individual soup bowls, and serve warm. Garnish each serving with a dollop of sour cream. Borscht may also be served chilled. Yield: about 3 cups.

*Sweet and Sour Cabbage Soup, a piquant, rib-sticking dish.*

## SWEET AND SOUR CABBAGE SOUP

3 pounds lean beef for stewing, cut into 1-inch cubes
1 soup bone
3 quarts water
1 large cabbage, shredded
3 large onions, thinly sliced
1 (16-ounce) can sauerkraut, undrained
2 (10-ounce) cans stewed tomatoes, undrained
2 (8-ounce) cans tomato sauce
1 cup firmly packed brown sugar
1½ teaspoons salt
1½ teaspoons pepper
½ cup vinegar

Combine beef, soup bone, and water in a large stockpot; bring to a boil. Reduce heat; cover and simmer 1½ hours.

Add remaining ingredients; simmer, uncovered, 1 hour, stirring occasionally. Remove and discard soup bone.

Ladle into soup bowls; serve warm. Yield: 2 gallons.

## SAUERKRAUT SOUP

1½ quarts water
2 tablespoons barley
4 medium potatoes, peeled and cubed
½ cup chopped onion
1 tablespoon bacon drippings
1 (10-ounce) can sauerkraut, undrained
1 tablespoon butter or margarine
2 tablespoons all-purpose flour
½ teaspoon salt
¼ teaspoon pepper

Combine water and barley in a large Dutch oven; cover and let stand 2 hours. Add potatoes, and bring to a boil. Reduce heat; simmer, uncovered, 15 minutes. Set aside.

Sauté onion in bacon drippings until tender; stir in sauerkraut. Cook over medium heat 15 minutes, stirring frequently. Stir sauerkraut mixture into reserved potato mixture, and set aside.

Melt butter in a small skillet over low heat; add flour, stirring until smooth. Cook over low heat, stirring constantly, until lightly browned. Add to sauerkraut mixture, mixing well. Stir in salt and pepper. Cook over medium heat, stirring frequently, until slightly thickened and thoroughly heated.

Serve soup immediately in warm soup bowls. Yield: 2½ quarts.

## COLLARD GREEN SOUP

1 (½-pound) ham bone or ham hock
¾ pound Spanish sausages or Chorizo, sliced
¼ pound salt pork, rinsed
1 quart water
1 (16-ounce) package frozen chopped collard greens
1 (16-ounce) can Great Northern beans, undrained
1 small onion, finely chopped
1 small green pepper, seeded and finely chopped
1 tablespoon bacon drippings
4 small red potatoes, peeled and diced
1 teaspoon salt
½ teaspoon pepper

Combine first 4 ingredients in a large Dutch oven. Bring to a boil. Reduce heat; cover and simmer 30 minutes. Add collard greens and beans; cover and simmer 30 minutes.

Sauté onion and green pepper in drippings until tender. Add sautéed vegetables, potatoes, salt, and pepper to collard green mixture; stir well. Cover; simmer 30 minutes or until vegetables are tender. Remove and discard ham bone and salt pork.

Spoon soup into individual bowls. Serve hot with cornbread, if desired. Yield: 2½ quarts.

*Young 4-H Club member shows his pleasure at winning a prize for his bushel of seed corn, c.1915.*

## CORN-PEANUT CHOWDER

½ cup chopped onion
2 tablespoons peanut oil
2 (17-ounce) cans cream-style corn
½ cup crunchy peanut butter
1 cup milk
1 teaspoon salt
¼ teaspoon pepper
1 cup (4 ounces) shredded sharp Cheddar cheese

Sauté onion in oil in a 3-quart saucepan until tender. Stir in corn and peanut butter. Cook over medium heat, stirring constantly, until bubbly. Stir in remaining ingredients; cook over medium heat, stirring constantly, until cheese melts and chowder is thoroughly heated.

Spoon chowder into individual serving bowls; serve immediately. Yield: 1½ quarts.

## SAVANNAH OKRA SOUP

2½ pounds bone-in beef shank
3 quarts water
2 (16-ounce) packages frozen cut okra
2 (29-ounce) cans stewed tomatoes, undrained
2 medium onions, chopped
2 teaspoons salt
½ teaspoon pepper
1 bay leaf
Hot cooked rice

Combine beef and water in a large Dutch oven. Bring to a boil. Reduce heat; cover and simmer 2 hours. Add next 6 ingredients; simmer, uncovered, 2 hours, stirring occasionally. Remove and discard bay leaf.

Serve soup immediately over hot cooked rice in individual soup bowls. Yield: 1 gallon.

Brown Brothers

## MUSHROOM AND BARLEY CHOWDER

1 medium onion, chopped
¼ cup butter or margarine
3 carrots, scraped and
chopped
1 cup diced celery
2 potatoes, peeled and
diced
1 pound fresh mushrooms,
sliced
½ cup barley
2 tablespoons chopped fresh
parsley
2 (10½-ounce) cans beef
broth, diluted
1 teaspoon salt

Sauté onion in butter in a
large Dutch oven until tender.
Add remaining ingredients,
stirring well. Cover and simmer
1½ hours or until vegetables
and barley are tender.
Serve chowder hot in individual bowls. Yield: about 2 quarts.

*Mushroom and Barley
Chowder. Barley is one
of the oldest and most
nutritious cereal grains.*

## GAZPACHO

3 medium tomatoes, peeled
and coarsely chopped
2 medium cucumbers, peeled
and coarsely chopped
1 medium-size green pepper,
seeded and coarsely
chopped
1 cup coarsely chopped celery
½ cup coarsely chopped
green onion
1 (46-ounce) can tomato juice
½ cup olive oil
¼ cup lemon juice
2 teaspoons salt
¼ teaspoon pepper
⅛ teaspoon hot sauce
Dash of garlic powder
Pinch of dried whole basil
Condiments

Combine first 13 ingredients
in a large bowl, mixing well.
Place one-fourth of mixture in
container of an electric blender;
process until almost smooth.
Repeat procedure with remaining mixture. Cover and chill at
least 3 hours. Transfer mixture
to a large glass pitcher or bowl.
Pour or ladle into individual
serving bowls.
On a tray, arrange bowls of
chopped green onion, chopped
cucumber, chopped green pepper, chopped celery, and croutons to be sprinkled over each
serving. Yield: 3 quarts.

Gazpacho has that
clean, direct taste of
utter freshness that
disarms us all. The Moors
brought the soup to Spain
longer ago than anyone remembers, and it is still the
pet of the Andalusians. Gazpacho takes its name from
the Arabic word meaning
"soaked bread," and the earliest form was little more
than water flavored with garlic and onions, with bread
put in to soak.

## LOLA'S GAZPACHO

3 (1-inch) slices French
bread, cubed
2 cloves garlic, quartered
¼ cup chopped green pepper
3 tablespoons water
½ teaspoon salt
¼ cup vegetable oil
2 large tomatoes, peeled and
quartered
¼ cup white wine vinegar
Ice cubes
Condiments

Combine bread cubes, garlic,
green pepper, water, and salt in
container of an electric blender;
process until smooth. Remove
cover; continue to process, adding oil in a thin steady stream.
Add tomatoes and vinegar; process until smooth. Cover and
chill thoroughly.
Pour Gazpacho into chilled individual serving bowls; place 1
ice cube in each serving. Serve
with several of the following
condiments: (about ½ cup each)
chopped cucumber, chopped tomato, chopped green pepper,
chopped green onion, chopped
hard-cooked egg, and croutons.
Yield: 3½ cups.

*In Lola's Gazpacho,
French bread is blended
smooth to give the soup
body; olive oil may be
substituted for vegetable oil.*

*Bowl of Summer Vegetable Soup and tureen of Spring Vegetable Soup surrounded by ingredients.*

## SPRING VEGETABLE SOUP

1 cup chopped leeks
1 green onion, chopped
2 tablespoons butter or margarine
1½ quarts hot water
2 medium potatoes, peeled, quartered, and thinly sliced
2 medium carrots, scraped and sliced
1 tablespoon salt
¼ cup uncooked regular rice
1 cup chopped fresh asparagus
½ pound fresh spinach, washed and finely chopped
1 cup half-and-half

Sauté leeks and onion in butter in a large Dutch oven until tender. Add water, potatoes, carrots, and salt. Bring to a boil. Reduce heat; cover and simmer 15 minutes. Stir in rice and asparagus; cover and simmer 20 minutes. Add spinach; cover and simmer an additional 10 minutes. Stir in half-and-half. Heat thoroughly, and ladle into individual soup bowls. Yield: 2 quarts.

## SUMMER VEGETABLE SOUP

3 cups water
1 cup peeled, diced potatoes
1 cup sliced carrots
2½ teaspoons salt
1 (16-ounce) package frozen green peas
1 cup fresh cauliflower flowerets
¼ pound fresh broccoli flowerets
3 tablespoons butter or margarine
3 tablespoons all-purpose flour
3 cups milk
¼ teaspoon white pepper
Chopped fresh parsley

Combine water, potatoes, carrots, and salt in a large saucepan; bring to a boil. Reduce heat; cover and simmer 10 minutes. Stir in peas, cauliflower, and broccoli; cover and simmer an additional 10 minutes or until vegetables are tender.

Melt butter in a small Dutch oven over low heat; add flour, stirring until smooth. Cook 1 minute, stirring constantly. Gradually add milk; cook over medium heat, stirring constantly, until thickened and bubbly. Stir in pepper. Gradually add vegetables and cooking liquid to white sauce, stirring well. Continue to cook, uncovered, over medium heat until thoroughly heated.

Ladle soup into individual bowls; sprinkle each with parsley. Serve warm. Yield: about 2½ quarts.

## VEGETABLE SOUP

1 (1¾-pound) meaty beef shank bone
5 quarts water
1 (28-ounce) can whole tomatoes, drained and coarsely chopped
3 cups lima beans
2 cups fresh corn cut from cob
½ medium-size head cabbage, coarsely grated
1 large baking potato, peeled and cubed
1 turnip, peeled, quartered, and sliced
2 carrots, scraped and sliced
1 cup chopped fresh parsley
½ cup chopped onion
4 dashes hot sauce
¼ cup firmly packed brown sugar
2 teaspoons salt
1 teaspoon pepper
3 tablespoons all-purpose flour

Combine shank bone and water in a large stockpot; bring to a boil. Skim surface, and reduce heat. Cover and simmer 5½ hours. Remove from heat. Cover and refrigerate overnight. Remove and discard excess fat. Strain broth through several layers of damp cheesecloth. Return broth to stockpot.

Bring broth to a boil; stir in remaining ingredients, except flour. Reduce heat; simmer, uncovered, 1 hour, stirring occasionally. Transfer ¾ cup soup to a small bowl; add flour, stirring to make a paste. Add flour mixture to soup in stockpot; stir until well blended. Return soup to a boil; cook, stirring constantly, until soup is slightly thickened.

Ladle into individual soup bowls, and serve warm. Yield: about 1½ gallons.

*A prize bull and his owner pose for the judges of a beef competition, c.1921. Beef for soup need not be so prime.*

## OXTAIL VEGETABLE SOUP

2 oxtails, cut into 2-inch pieces
2 (14½-ounce) cans whole tomatoes, undrained
1 (16-ounce) can cut okra, undrained
2 cups vegetable cocktail juice
4 carrots, scraped and thinly sliced
4 stalks celery, cleaned and thinly sliced
3 medium onions, chopped
¼ large head cabbage, coarsely chopped
½ pound fresh green beans, snapped and strings removed
1 cup water
¾ cup barley
1 tablespoon sugar
2 teaspoons salt
½ teaspoon pepper

Combine all ingredients in a large stockpot; bring to a boil. Reduce heat; cover and simmer 3 hours.

Remove oxtails. Remove meat; coarsely chop, discarding bones. Add meat to soup.

Ladle soup into individual serving bowls; serve warm. Yield: about 5 quarts.

## HOMEMADE VEGETABLE-BEEF SOUP

1 pound lean beef for stewing, cut into ½-inch cubes
2 tablespoons shortening
1 quart boiling water
1 (28-ounce) can whole tomatoes, undrained and chopped
½ cup chopped onion
1 celery stalk with leaves, cleaned and chopped
1 tablespoon salt
¼ teaspoon pepper
¼ cup uncooked brown rice (optional)
5 medium carrots, scraped and sliced
3 medium potatoes, peeled and cubed

Brown meat in shortening in a large Dutch oven. Add water, tomatoes, onion, celery, salt, pepper, and brown rice, if desired; bring mixture to a boil. Reduce heat; cover and simmer 3 hours. Add carrots and potatoes; stir well. Cover and cook over medium heat an additional 15 minutes or until vegetables are tender.

Ladle soup into individual bowls; serve warm. Yield: 3 quarts.

## MINESTRONE

1½ pounds lean ground
   chuck
1 egg, well beaten
½ cup cooking sherry, divided
1 lemon
2 tablespoons Italian
   seasoning
1½ teaspoons salt
½ teaspoon pepper
1 (4- to 5-pound) baking hen
2 large onions, chopped
2 small green peppers, seeded
   and chopped
1 large celery stalk with
   leaves, cleaned and chopped
¼ cup barley
1 medium-size red pepper
   pod, chopped
3 cloves garlic
1½ tablespoons chicken-
   flavored bouillon granules
1 bay leaf
1 (29-ounce) can whole
   tomatoes, undrained and
   chopped
2 medium turnips, peeled and
   diced
1 cup chopped fresh
   mushrooms
1 (29-ounce) can cut green
   beans, undrained
1 (28-ounce) can whole kernel
   corn, undrained
1 (17-ounce) can green peas,
   undrained
1 (16-ounce) can sliced
   carrots, undrained
1 (8-ounce) can sliced water
   chestnuts, undrained
¼ cup chopped fresh dillweed
¼ cup chopped fresh parsley
1 (8-ounce) package
   fettuccine, broken into
   ½-inch pieces
Grated Parmesan cheese
Chopped fresh chives

Combine meat, egg, ¼ cup cooking sherry, juice of lemon (reserve rind), Italian seasoning, salt, and pepper in a medium mixing bowl; mix well. Cover tightly, and refrigerate mixture overnight. Shape into ½-inch meatballs, and refrigerate until ready to use.

Remove giblets from hen; reserve for other uses. Remove excess fat from hen; discard. Rinse hen in cold water.

Combine prepared hen, onion, green pepper, celery, barley, remaining cooking sherry, red pepper, garlic, bouillon granules, bay leaf, and reserved lemon rind in a 21-quart stockpot. Add water to cover hen; stir well. Cover and bring to a boil. Reduce heat to medium, and cook 1 hour.

Remove garlic and bay leaf from broth with a slotted spoon, and discard. Remove hen from broth, and cool slightly. Bone hen, and chop meat. Discard bones; return meat to broth. Stir in tomatoes, turnips, and mushrooms. Bring to a boil.

Add reserved meatballs, one at a time, to boiling broth; stir well. Add green beans, corn, peas, carrots, and water chestnuts, stirring well after each addition. Stir in dillweed, parsley, and fettuccine. Cover and remove from heat. Let soup stand 1 hour.

Ladle soup into individual bowls; sprinkle each serving with Parmesan cheese and chopped fresh chives. Serve warm. Yield: 5 gallons.

*Note:* Minestrone freezes well.

## SOUTHERN JUGGED SOUP

6 medium potatoes, peeled
   and sliced
6 tomatoes, peeled and
   coarsely chopped
1 medium onion, thinly sliced
1 turnip, peeled and diced
2 large carrots, sliced
2½ cups frozen green peas
¼ cup uncooked regular rice
1 tablespoon sugar
1 tablespoon salt
½ teaspoon pepper
Dash of ground allspice
2 quarts beef broth

Layer potatoes, tomatoes, onion, turnip, carrots, peas, and rice in a 5-quart casserole; sprinkle sugar, salt, pepper, and allspice over vegetables. Pour broth over vegetables.

Cover tightly, and bake at 300° for 5 hours. Remove from oven, and ladle into individual serving bowls; serve hot. Yield: about 5 quarts.

## ONE-DISH SUPPER SOUP

1 cup chopped celery
2 small onions, chopped
1 green pepper, seeded and
   chopped
1 tablespoon butter or
   margarine
3 cups boiling water
2 cups chopped, peeled
   tomatoes
½ teaspoon salt
6 eggs
Salt and pepper to taste
1 cup (4 ounces) shredded
   sharp Cheddar cheese
Hot cooked rice

Sauté celery, onion, and green pepper in butter in a 4-quart Dutch oven until tender. Stir in boiling water, tomato, and salt, mixing well. Simmer, uncovered, 15 minutes. Carefully break eggs into hot soup. (Do not stir.) Add salt and pepper.

Sprinkle cheese over egg and soup mixture. Cover; simmer 5 minutes. Serve immediately over rice in individual soup bowls. Yield: 6 servings.

*Vegetables overflow on the cover of Burpee's 1888 seed catalogue.*

# HEARTY FARE

O ur soups to this point have been spoonable, even drinkable. Now come the true rib-stickers: fiery chilies, toothsome jambalayas, and gumbos served on beds of — what else? — rice. And those soul-satisfying stews so solid with good things that a spoon will almost stand alone in the bowl.

Purists rightly insist that chili, in the first place, was a dish of cubed beef or venison, cooked ever so tender, seasoned on the high side with chili pepper, with only enough water to keep it from sticking to the pot. Trail cooks took pride in its preparation. Cowboys were terribly particular about their chili because, living mostly on beans, biscuits, and coffee, they hungered for beef. Beans and chopped onions were legal only as side dishes. Chili has been institutionalized in Texas, and the cook-off that began at Terlingua still brings in contestants from many countries.

It was rice from the Orient that gave the South its alternative to grits; few meals will omit both grains. Rice came to the marshes of the Low Country in 1694, and Louisiana, Texas, and Arkansas joined in making it a staple and a cash crop. Farmers in the Louisiana bayous now do some interesting double-cropping. They harvest rice in the fall, then flood the fields and, in March, start pulling in tons of crayfish: two foundations of the Cajun diet.

Gumbos and jambalayas may contain one or more kinds of seafood, chicken, or other poultry, or combinations of pork, seafood, and sausage. Gumbos are served over rice; in jambalayas, rice is an ingredient. Ask about gumbo in Cajun country around, say, Breaux Bridge, The "Crawfish" Capital of the World. "First you make a roux," they'll say, but that doesn't hold true throughout the South. Gumbo contains okra, famed for its almost gelatinous thickening power. Gumbo filé means that filé powder is used instead of or along with okra as thickener and flavor agent.

Nothing could be more typical of the South's beginnings than stews. Having sometimes only one kettle and certainly no forks, colonists literally lived on stews. Brunswick or Pine Bark or Burgoo . . . they're all part of the family.

*Brunswick Stew (front) once made with squirrel instead of chicken. Jambalaya of Chicken (back) developed after rice crops were established in the Low Country.*

# THE CHILI COLLECTION

*Beef canning company trade card, c.1890, shows premium cattle on the hoof.*

## TEXAS CHILI

3 pounds chili-ground
    beef
3 large onions, chopped
½ cup all-purpose flour
1 (10½-ounce) can beef
    consommé, undiluted
¼ cup plus 2 tablespoons
    chili powder
1 tablespoon salt
1 tablespoon ground cumin
1½ teaspoons ground
    oregano
Shredded Cheddar cheese

Combine ground beef and onion in a large Dutch oven; cook until meat is browned, stirring to crumble meat. Drain off pan drippings. Stir in flour; cook 2 minutes, stirring constantly. Gradually add consommé, stirring constantly. Stir in chili powder, salt, cumin, and oregano. Simmer, uncovered, 30 minutes or until thickened, stirring occasionally.

Ladle chili into individual serving bowls, and sprinkle with cheese. Yield: 2 quarts.

## TEXAS CHAMPIONSHIP CHILI

2 large onions, chopped
3 cloves garlic, minced
1 jalapeño pepper, finely
    chopped
1 tablespoon peanut oil
3 pounds boneless chuck
    roast, finely diced
1 teaspoon cumin seeds
1½ tablespoons oregano
1 (1½-ounce) can chili powder
1 (28-ounce) can whole
    tomatoes, undrained
3½ cups water
Shredded Cheddar cheese

Sauté first 3 ingredients in oil until tender; set aside.

Combine meat, cumin, and oregano in a large Dutch oven; cook over medium heat until meat is browned. Add onion mixture, chili powder, tomatoes, and water; bring to a boil. Reduce heat; cover and simmer 2 to 3 hours, stirring frequently.

Ladle into individual soup bowls. Top each serving with cheese. Yield: about 1½ quarts.

## CHILI CON CARNE

2 pounds lean beef for
    stewing, cut into 1-inch
    cubes
3 tablespoons all-purpose
    flour
2 tablespoons chili powder
2 cloves garlic, minced
1 large onion, chopped
2 tablespoons suet
1 tablespoon vegetable oil
1 quart hot water
2 teaspoons salt
1 (15-ounce) can chili beans,
    undrained

Combine first 4 ingredients in a large bowl; set aside.

Sauté onion in suet and oil in a large Dutch oven until tender. Add meat mixture; mix well. Simmer 15 minutes, stirring frequently. Gradually add water, stirring constantly; stir in salt. Simmer, uncovered, 1½ hours or until meat is tender. Stir in beans; heat thoroughly.

Ladle into individual serving bowls, and serve immediately. Yield: about 2 quarts.

## MEATY CHILI

2 pounds ground beef
½ cup chopped onion
½ cup chopped celery
2 (16-ounce) cans red kidney beans, undrained
2 (10¾-ounce) cans tomato puree
2 (8-ounce) cans tomato sauce
3 tablespoons chili powder
2 teaspoons salt
1 teaspoon garlic salt
1 teaspoon sugar

Combine ground beef, onion, and celery in a large Dutch oven; cook over medium heat until meat is browned, stirring to crumble meat. Drain off pan drippings. Stir in remaining ingredients. Bring to a boil. Reduce heat; cover and simmer 2 hours, stirring occasionally.

Ladle chili into individual serving bowls, and serve immediately. Yield: 2 quarts.

## EASY HEARTY CHILI

2 pounds ground beef
1 medium onion, chopped
3 cloves garlic, minced
3 cups water
1 (16-ounce) can whole tomatoes, undrained and chopped
1 (8-ounce) can tomato sauce
2 tablespoons all-purpose flour
1½ teaspoons salt
½ teaspoon sugar
3 tablespoons chili powder
1 teaspoon ground cumin
½ teaspoon dried whole oregano
½ teaspoon dried whole basil
Dash of red pepper
1 (16-ounce) can pinto beans, undrained

Combine ground beef, onion, and garlic in a large Dutch oven; cook until meat is browned, stirring to crumble meat. Drain off pan drippings. Add water, tomatoes, tomato sauce, flour, salt, sugar, chili powder, cumin, oregano, basil, and pepper, mixing well. Cover and simmer 1½ hours, stirring occasionally. Add pinto beans, and simmer an additional 30 minutes.

Ladle into individual bowls, and serve immediately. Yield: 3 quarts.

The most widely used chili powder in the world is Gebhardt's, invented by a German from New Braunfels, Texas. He opened a cafe in San Antonio in 1890. Seeing his Mexican dishes outsell the others, he evolved a seasoning of ancho chiles, cumin, and other spices: the Mexican seasoning industry was born.

*William Gebhardt (center) and friends toast Gebhardt's Chili Powder.*

*Cold Weather Chili is one of the best, made with pinto beans and some pork mixed in with the beef.*

## COLD WEATHER CHILI

½ (16-ounce) package dried pinto beans
1½ quarts water
5 (16-ounce) cans whole tomatoes, undrained
2½ pounds lean ground beef
1 pound lean ground pork
3 medium-size green peppers, seeded and chopped
1 large onion, chopped
1 clove garlic, crushed
½ cup chopped fresh parsley
⅓ cup chili powder
1½ teaspoons cumin seeds
2 tablespoons salt
1½ teaspoons pepper

Sort and wash beans; place in a large Dutch oven. Add water; let soak overnight. Bring to a boil. Reduce heat; cover and simmer 2½ hours or until beans are tender. Add tomatoes; cover and simmer 5 minutes.

Sauté meat, green pepper, onion, and garlic in a large skillet 15 minutes or until vegetables are tender. Stir in parsley and chili powder; simmer 15 minutes.

Add meat mixture to Dutch oven; stir in cumin, salt, and pepper. Bring to a boil. Reduce heat; cover and simmer 1 hour. Uncover and cook over medium heat an additional 30 minutes.

Ladle into a large serving dish or individual soup bowls; serve immediately. Yield: 1 gallon.

# PRIZE-WINNING SPICY CHILI

1 pound boneless chuck roast, cut into ¼-inch cubes
1 pound lean ground beef
1 pound bulk pork sausage
1½ cups chopped green pepper
1½ cups chopped onion
2 tablespoons minced garlic
1 to 2 jalapeño peppers, finely chopped
¼ cup plus 1 tablespoon chili powder
1 teaspoon salt
2½ teaspoons ground cumin
2 teaspoons cocoa
¼ teaspoon pepper
2 bay leaves
2 (10½-ounce) cans beef broth, undiluted
3 (16-ounce) cans Italian-style tomatoes, drained and chopped
1 (6-ounce) can tomato paste
1 (16-ounce) can red kidney beans, drained
1 cup beer
Commercial sour cream
Finely chopped zucchini
Chopped green onion

Combine meat in a large Dutch oven; cook over medium heat, stirring frequently, until meat is browned. Remove meat with a slotted spoon, reserving drippings in Dutch oven. Set meat aside.

Sauté green pepper, 1½ cups chopped onion, and garlic in drippings in Dutch oven 10 minutes or until tender. Drain off drippings.

Add meat, jalapeño pepper, chili powder, salt, cumin, cocoa, pepper, and bay leaves to Dutch oven; stir until blended. Add beef broth, tomatoes, and tomato paste, stirring well; bring to a boil. Reduce heat; simmer, uncovered, 25 minutes or until mixture begins to thicken, stirring occasionally.

Add kidney beans to mixture; simmer, uncovered, an additional 15 minutes. Remove from heat, and cool to room temperature; discard bay leaves. Cover and refrigerate overnight to allow flavors to blend.

Place chili over medium heat; cook, uncovered until thoroughly heated, stirring occasionally. Stir in beer, and heat thoroughly.

Ladle chili into individual serving bowls. Garnish each serving with a dollop of sour cream; sprinkle with zucchini and green onion. Serve immediately. Yield: about 3 quarts.

## VENISON CHILI

1 pound chili-ground venison
1 pound chili-ground chuck
1 medium onion, chopped
2 cloves garlic, chopped
1 cup catsup
1 (8-ounce) can tomato sauce
3 tablespoons chili powder
2 teaspoons salt
¼ teaspoon ground cumin
¼ teaspoon pepper
Red pepper to taste
1 quart water

Combine meat, onion, and garlic in a small Dutch oven; cook over medium heat until meat is browned, stirring to crumble meat. Drain off pan drippings. Add remaining ingredients, mixing well. Cover and simmer 3 hours, stirring occasionally.

Ladle into individual serving bowls, and serve immediately. Yield: about 2 quarts.

# GUMBOS AND JAMBALAYAS

## GUMBO Z'HERBES

1 pound collard greens, cleaned and chopped
1 pound turnip greens, cleaned and chopped
1 pound spinach, cleaned and chopped
1 bunch watercress, cleaned and chopped
1 bunch carrot tops, cleaned and chopped
1 bunch fresh parsley, chopped
1 small cabbage, chopped
½ bunch green onions, chopped
1 gallon water
¼ cup shortening
¼ cup all-purpose flour
1 large onion, chopped
1 pound fully cooked ham, diced
½ pound smoked sausage links, cubed
2 bay leaves
1 teaspoon dried whole thyme
2 teaspoons salt
½ teaspoon pepper
¼ teaspoon red pepper
¼ teaspoon ground allspice
Hot cooked rice

Combine first 9 ingredients in a large stockpot; bring to a boil. Reduce heat; simmer, uncovered, 2 hours. Strain mixture, reserving greens and liquid. Set each aside.

Melt shortening in a large Dutch oven; add flour, stirring until well blended. Cook over medium heat, stirring constantly, 30 minutes or until roux is the color of a copper penny. Stir in onion, ham, and sausage; cook 5 minutes. Add reserved greens; cook 5 minutes, stirring constantly. Stir in reserved liquid and remaining ingredients, except rice. Simmer, uncovered, 1 hour. Remove and discard bay leaves.

Serve gumbo over hot cooked rice in individual bowls. Yield: 1 gallon.

The American South is the undisputed home of certain world-class comestibles. The French may have their bouillabaisse, the Italians their cioppino, but seafood gumbos are to be had only in the Southeast United States. That is where okra landed from Africa and where the Choctaws made filé powder. The Chinese gave us rice, but not the princely jambalayas with the rice cooked in, a divinely inspired arrangement of give-and-take in flavor and texture. These dishes are among those that give us our inordinate pride in our regionality. Pardonable pride, we believe.

## BEEF AND HAM GUMBO

¾ pound chopped, cooked ham
1 pound lean beef for stewing, cut into 1-inch cubes
1 medium onion, sliced
1 medium-size green pepper, seeded and finely chopped
½ cup chopped celery
2 tablespoons chopped fresh parsley
1 (28-ounce) can whole tomatoes, undrained and chopped
2 cups water
1 quart sliced okra
1 bay leaf
1 teaspoon salt
½ teaspoon celery salt
½ teaspoon pepper
Hot cooked rice

Sauté meat in a large Dutch oven until browned. Stir in onion, green pepper, celery, and parsley; cook until vegetables are tender. Add tomatoes and water; mix well, and bring to a boil. Reduce heat; cover and simmer 1½ hours or until meat is tender.

Add okra, bay leaf, and seasonings to Dutch oven, stirring well. Simmer, uncovered, an additional 1½ hours or until okra is tender and gumbo has thickened, stirring occasionally. Remove and discard bay leaf.

Ladle gumbo over hot cooked rice in individual serving bowls. Yield: about 2 quarts.

## CREOLE CHICKEN GUMBO

1 (3- to 3½-pound) broiler-fryer, cut up
2 teaspoons salt
¼ teaspoon pepper
2 tablespoons butter or margarine
2 cups diced cooked ham
1 small onion, minced
1 small green pepper, seeded and minced
1½ quarts boiling water
1 (14½-ounce) can whole tomatoes, undrained and chopped
3 cups sliced okra
3 bay leaves
1 teaspoon chopped fresh thyme
1 teaspoon creole seasoning
¼ teaspoon red pepper
Hot cooked rice

Sprinkle chicken with salt and pepper; set aside.

Melt butter in a large stockpot over medium heat; add chicken and ham. Reduce heat; cover and simmer 10 minutes. Add onion and green pepper; continue cooking until vegetables are tender. Stir in next 7 ingredients. Bring mixture to a boil. Reduce heat; simmer, uncovered, 2 hours, stirring occasionally. Remove and discard bay leaves.

Ladle gumbo into serving dish; serve immediately over rice in individual serving bowls. Yield: about 1 gallon.

Stained glass courtesy of the Class Glass Studio, Montgomery, Alabama

*Beef and Ham Gumbo (front) and tureen of Creole Chicken Gumbo.*

## CHICKEN GUMBO FILÉ

1 (5-pound) stewing hen,
  cut up
¾ cup plus 2 tablespoons
  vegetable oil
¼ cup plus 2 tablespoons
  all-purpose flour
1½ cups chopped onion
3 quarts water
1 tablespoon salt
1½ teaspoons pepper
1 (12-ounce) container
  Standard oysters, drained
2 tablespoons chopped fresh
  parsley
2 tablespoons chopped green
  onion tops
2 teaspoons filé powder
Hot cooked rice

Brown chicken in hot oil in a large stockpot. Remove chicken and set aside, reserving pan drippings in stockpot.

Add flour to pan drippings; cook over low heat, stirring constantly, 50 minutes or until roux is the color of a copper penny. Add chopped onion, and cook 1 minute, stirring constantly.

Gradually add 3 quarts water to roux, stirring until well blended. Add reserved chicken, salt, and pepper. Bring mixture to a boil. Reduce heat, and simmer, uncovered, 2 hours, stirring occasionally.

Add oysters and simmer, uncovered, 5 minutes; stir in parsley and onion tops and cook an additional 5 minutes. Remove from heat.

Stir in filé powder to thicken gumbo. Ladle gumbo over hot cooked rice in individual serving bowls and serve immediately. Yield: about 1 gallon.

Brown Breasted Red Game, *by J. Porter, painted for* Poultry World *in 1877.*

The Historic New Orleans Collection, 533 Royal Street

## DUCK GUMBO

3 (3½- to 4-pound) dressed
  ducklings, skinned and
  cut up
2 teaspoons salt, divided
¾ cup vegetable oil, divided
½ cup all-purpose flour
1 cup chopped onion
¾ cup chopped green onion
3 quarts water
1 (10-ounce) package frozen
  okra, thawed
½ teaspoon hot sauce
¼ teaspoon red pepper
¼ cup chopped fresh parsley
2 cloves garlic, minced
½ pound smoked sausage, cut
  into ½-inch pieces
Hot cooked rice

Sprinkle ducklings with 1 teaspoon salt; brown in ¼ cup hot oil in a large skillet over medium heat, turning to brown evenly. Drain well, and set aside.

Combine remaining oil and flour in a large stockpot; cook over medium heat, stirring constantly, 45 minutes or until roux is the color of a copper penny. Add onion, and continue cooking until tender.

Gradually add water, stirring until well blended. Add duckling, okra, hot sauce, remaining salt, and red pepper. Simmer, uncovered, 2½ hours or until meat begins to fall off bones. Remove from heat; cool. Cover; refrigerate overnight.

Skim off and discard fat from surface. Remove duckling; remove meat from bones, discarding bones. Coarsely chop meat; return to gumbo.

Add parsley, garlic, and sausage. Cook over low heat until thoroughly heated.

Ladle gumbo over rice in individual serving bowls; serve immediately. Yield: 1 gallon.

Collection of Business Americana

New Orleans' French Market, *drawing of Indians selling gumbo filé by Frank H. Taylor, 1870.*

## TURKEY-SAUSAGE GUMBO

1 turkey carcass
1 gallon water, divided
4 cups chopped, cooked turkey
½ cup vegetable oil
½ cup bacon drippings
1 cup all-purpose flour
8 stalks celery, chopped
3 large onions, chopped
1 small green pepper, seeded and chopped
2 cloves garlic, minced
½ cup chopped fresh parsley
1 pound okra, cleaned and sliced
½ pound smoked sausage, cut into ¼-inch slices
1 (14½-ounce) can whole tomatoes, undrained and chopped
½ cup Worcestershire sauce
4 slices bacon, cut into 1-inch pieces
1½ teaspoons salt
½ teaspoon hot sauce
¼ teaspoon red pepper
2 bay leaves
1 tablespoon lemon juice
1 teaspoon firmly packed brown sugar
Hot cooked rice

Crack turkey carcass. Combine carcass and 3 quarts water in a large stockpot; bring to a boil. Reduce heat; cover and simmer 1 hour.

Remove carcass from stock; set stock aside. Remove any meat remaining on bones; discard bones. Chop meat into bite-size pieces, and combine with chopped turkey; cover and refrigerate.

Combine oil, bacon drippings, and flour in a large stockpot; stir until well blended. Cook over medium heat, stirring frequently, until roux is the color of a copper penny. Stir in celery, onion, green pepper, garlic, and parsley; cook over low heat 20 minutes, stirring frequently. Add okra and sausage; cook an additional 5 minutes, stirring frequently.

Add reserved turkey stock, remaining water, tomatoes, Worcestershire sauce, bacon, salt, hot sauce, red pepper, and bay leaves; simmer, uncovered, 2½ hours, stirring occasionally. Stir in reserved turkey, and

cook, uncovered, an additional 30 minutes. Remove and discard bay leaves. Stir in lemon juice and brown sugar.

Ladle gumbo over hot cooked rice in individual bowls and serve immediately. Yield: 5 quarts.

Gumbo is a satisfying dish, and that is one of the few flat statements to be made on the subject. We expect gumbo to contain the basic "copper penny"-colored dark roux plus okra or filé powder, that famous Indian seasoning made of sassafras leaves. Our Crab Gumbo (page 118) does contain okra but is not based on the roux. Gumbo z'Herbes, based on a dark roux, originated as a Lenten dish with seven kinds of greens for luck!

## CRAB GUMBO

1 medium onion, chopped
1 stalk celery, chopped
1 clove garlic, minced
¼ cup butter or margarine
3 (14½-ounce) cans whole
  tomatoes, undrained and
  chopped
1 (10-ounce) package frozen
  cut okra, thawed
1 bay leaf
2 teaspoons salt
1 teaspoon sugar
½ teaspoon dried whole
  thyme
¼ teaspoon chili powder
¼ teaspoon pepper
1 pound lump crabmeat,
  drained
Hot cooked rice

Sauté onion, celery, and garlic in butter in a large stockpot until tender. Add next 8 ingredients; bring to boil. Reduce heat; cover and simmer 1 hour. Stir in crabmeat; cook over low heat until thoroughly heated. Remove and discard bay leaf.

Ladle gumbo over hot cooked rice in individual bowls and serve immediately. Yield: 1½ quarts.

## OYSTER GUMBO

2 tablespoons butter or
  margarine
1 (4-pound) stewing hen,
  cut up
½ pound fully cooked ham,
  cut into ½-inch cubes
2 large onions, chopped
¼ red pepper pod, seeded
2 teaspoons creole seasoning
1 teaspoon salt
½ teaspoon garlic salt
1 quart water
3 (12-ounce) containers
  Standard oysters, undrained
Filé powder
Hot cooked rice

Melt butter in a large Dutch oven; add chicken and ham. Cover and cook over medium heat 10 minutes, turning to brown all sides. Add onion, pepper, creole seasoning, salt, and garlic salt; cook 5 minutes, stirring constantly. Add water.

Drain oysters, reserving oyster liquor; set oysters aside. Stir liquor into chicken mixture; bring to a boil. Reduce heat; cover and simmer 1½ hours or until chicken is tender.

Remove chicken from broth, and cool. Bone chicken, and chop meat into bite-size pieces; discard bones. Return meat to broth. Bring to a boil. Stir in reserved oysters, and cook 3 minutes or until oyster edges begin to curl.

Stir in filé powder to taste just before serving. Serve gumbo over rice in individual bowls. Yield: 2½ quarts.

*"Creole" brand oyster label from a Houma, Louisiana, packer.*

*"Martina's Oysters" delivery truck, of 1920 vintage, pictured in New Orleans.*

## SEAFOOD GUMBO

¼ cup butter or margarine
¼ cup all-purpose flour
2 quarts water
2 pounds okra, cleaned and sliced
3 (14½-ounce) cans whole tomatoes, undrained and chopped
1 medium onion, chopped
1½ teaspoons salt
½ teaspoon pepper
½ teaspoon red pepper
½ teaspoon garlic powder
½ teaspoon dried whole thyme
½ teaspoon creole seasoning
2 pounds uncooked medium shrimp, peeled and deveined
1 pound lump or flake crabmeat, drained
1 pound red snapper fillets, cut into 1-inch cubes
1 (12-ounce) container Standard oysters, drained
Hot cooked rice

Melt butter in a large stockpot over low heat; add flour, stirring until smooth. Cook over medium heat, stirring constantly, until roux is the color of a copper penny. Add water, okra, tomatoes, onion, salt, pepper, garlic powder, thyme, and creole seasoning; bring mixture to a boil. Reduce heat, and simmer 1 hour.

Add remaining ingredients, except rice, and simmer, uncovered, an additional 15 minutes, stirring frequently.

Serve gumbo over hot cooked rice in individual bowls. Yield: about 1 gallon.

## LOUISIANA GUMBO

2 (16-ounce) packages frozen cut okra, thawed
2 medium onions, chopped
2 tablespoons vegetable oil
7 cups water
4 cups cubed, fully cooked ham
2 bay leaves
1 tablespoon salt
½ teaspoon pepper
¼ teaspoon dried whole thyme
2 pounds uncooked medium shrimp, peeled and deveined
1 (12-ounce) container Standard oysters, drained
Hot cooked rice

Sauté okra and onion in oil in a large Dutch oven until tender and lightly browned. Add next 6 ingredients; bring to a boil. Reduce heat; simmer, uncovered, 1 hour. Stir in shrimp and oysters; cook, uncovered, an additional 10 minutes. Remove and discard bay leaves.

Serve gumbo over hot cooked rice in individual bowls. Yield: 2½ quarts.

*Cajun Gumbo, filled with chicken, sausage, and three kinds of seafood, can't fail to please every palate.*

## CAJUN GUMBO

1 pound fully cooked Klobase sausage
2 medium-size green peppers, seeded and chopped
1 large onion, chopped
1 stalk celery, chopped
4 cloves garlic, chopped
½ cup plus 2 tablespoons butter or margarine, divided
1 (2- to 2½-pound) broiler-fryer, cut up
½ cup all-purpose flour
1 (10¾-ounce) can chicken broth, undiluted
¼ cup chopped fresh parsley
⅛ teaspoon dried whole thyme
⅛ teaspoon dried whole oregano
⅛ teaspoon dried whole basil
⅛ teaspoon ground cumin
⅛ teaspoon dried whole tarragon
1½ quarts water
½ pound uncooked medium shrimp, peeled and deveined
1 (12-ounce) container Standard oysters, drained
½ cup flake crabmeat
7 green onions, sliced
¼ cup tomato paste
1 bay leaf
1½ teaspoons salt
½ teaspoon pepper
½ teaspoon hot sauce
Hot cooked rice

Cut sausage into ½-inch slices. Place sausage and water to cover in a large skillet; bring to a boil. Reduce heat; cover and cook 10 minutes or until thoroughly heated. Remove from heat; drain well, and set aside.

Sauté green pepper, chopped onion, celery, and garlic in 2 tablespoons butter in a large stockpot until tender. Add chicken, and cook until browned on all sides; remove from heat, and set aside.

Melt remaining butter in a large skillet over low heat; add flour, stirring until smooth. Cook over medium heat, stirring frequently, 45 minutes or until roux is the color of a copper penny. Add chicken broth, parsley, thyme, oregano, basil, cumin, and tarragon; stir until well blended.

Add roux mixture, water, shrimp, oysters, crabmeat, green onion, tomato paste, bay leaf, and reserved sausage to sautéed vegetables and chicken in stockpot; stir until well blended. Bring to a boil. Reduce heat, and simmer, uncovered, 1 hour.

Remove chicken from gumbo; cool. Remove chicken from bones; cut meat into bite-size pieces, and return to gumbo. Remove and discard bay leaf. Stir in salt, pepper, and hot sauce.

Serve gumbo immediately over hot cooked rice in individual serving bowls. Yield: about 2½ quarts.

# OYSTER CREOLE

2 (12-ounce) containers
  Standard oysters, undrained
1 cup chopped fresh
  mushrooms
½ cup chopped celery
¼ cup chopped green pepper
¼ cup butter or margarine
2 (14½-ounce) cans whole
  tomatoes, undrained and
  chopped
2 tablespoons dried minced
  onion
½ teaspoon sugar
½ teaspoon salt
½ teaspoon lemon-pepper
  seasoning
¼ teaspoon chili powder
¼ teaspoon dried whole
  tarragon
¼ teaspoon hot sauce
Red pepper to taste
2 tablespoons cornstarch
2 tablespoons water
Hot cooked rice

Drain oysters, reserving liquor; set aside.

Sauté mushrooms, celery, and green pepper in butter in a large saucepan until tender. Stir in reserved oyster liquor, tomatoes, and next 8 ingredients; bring to a boil. Reduce heat; cover and simmer 30 minutes.

Combine cornstarch and water; mix well. Gradually add to tomato mixture; stir well. Bring to a boil. Reduce heat; stir in oysters. Simmer, uncovered, until oyster edges curl.

Spoon over hot cooked rice in individual serving bowls. Yield: about 1 quart.

---

Oyster Creole falls somewhere between gumbo and jambalaya. It meets the criteria for neither, yet belongs near gumbo because it is rich in oysters, comes with thickened gravy, and goes over rice. It is a Maryland dish, one of a class that uses "Creole" in the title because of the tomatoes in it.

---

# PORK JAMBALAYA

1 pound pork, cut into 1-inch
  cubes
3 medium onions, finely
  chopped
2 tablespoons shortening
1 pound chopped cooked ham
½ pound smoked sausage, cut
  into bite-size pieces
3 (10¾-ounce) cans beef
  broth, undiluted
1 bay leaf
1 sprig fresh parsley
2 whole cloves
½ teaspoon salt
1 cup uncooked regular rice
1 tablespoon chili sauce
¼ teaspoon hot sauce
Dash of red pepper

Sauté pork and onion in shortening in a large Dutch oven 5 minutes. Stir in ham and sausage; cook until meat is browned. Add beef broth, bay leaf, parsley, cloves, and salt.

Bring to a boil. Reduce heat; simmer, uncovered, 10 minutes. Gradually stir in rice. Cover and cook over medium heat, stirring frequently, until meat and rice are tender. Stir in remaining ingredients. Remove bay leaf and cloves; discard.

Serve immediately in individual bowls. Yield: about 3½ quarts.

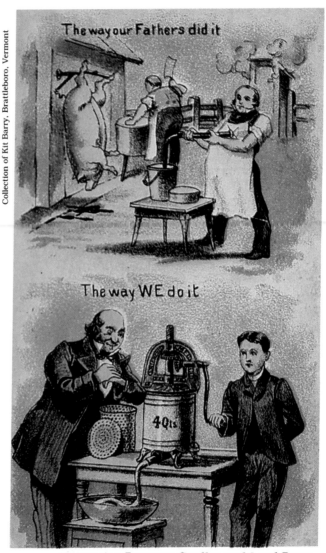

Collection of Kit Barry, Brattleboro, Vermont

*Enterprise Sausage Stuffer and Lard Press.*

## JAMBALAYA OF CHICKEN

¼ cup lard or shortening
1 (3-pound) broiler-fryer,
  cut up
¾ pound cubed cooked ham
1 medium onion, chopped
1 medium-size green pepper,
  seeded and chopped
3 cloves garlic, minced
1¼ cups uncooked regular
  rice
2 quarts water
1 tomato, peeled and chopped
¼ cup chopped fresh parsley
1½ tablespoons salt
1½ teaspoons pepper
1 teaspoon dried whole thyme
1 teaspoon hot sauce
3 bay leaves
¼ teaspoon dried whole basil
¼ teaspoon dried whole
  oregano

Melt lard in a small stockpot
over medium heat; add chicken
and ham, and cook, turning to
brown all sides. Remove chicken
and ham; set aside, reserving
pan drippings. Add onion,
green pepper, and garlic to pan
drippings; sauté until tender.
Stir in rice; cook over medium
heat until rice is browned.

Add water, tomato, parsley,
salt, pepper, thyme, hot sauce,
bay leaves, basil, oregano, and
reserved chicken and ham;
bring to a boil. Reduce heat;
simmer, uncovered, 1½ hours,
stirring frequently. Remove and
discard bay leaves.

Transfer pieces of chicken to
individual serving plates. Spoon
jambalaya over chicken, and
serve immediately. Yield: about
3 quarts.

*"The Old French Market
in New Orleans on
Sunday Morning," by
C. Upham, in* Leslie's
Illustrated Newspaper, *1883.*

## SHRIMP AND OYSTER JAMBALAYA

3 large onions, chopped
3 large green peppers, seeded and chopped
3 stalks celery, cleaned and chopped
3 cloves garlic, chopped
½ cup shortening
2 (6-ounce) cans tomato paste
1 cup water
Salt and pepper to taste
3 (12-ounce) containers Standard oysters, drained
2 pounds uncooked medium shrimp, peeled and deveined
2 cups cooked regular rice

Sauté onion, green pepper, celery, and garlic in shortening until tender. Stir in tomato paste, water, and salt and pepper; bring to a boil. Reduce heat; cover and simmer 2 hours.

Return mixture to a boil; stir in oysters and shrimp. Cook, uncovered, 5 minutes or until shrimp are tender and oyster edges curl. Stir in rice.

Spoon jambalaya into individual bowls; serve warm. Yield: about 2 quarts.

## CRAYFISH ÉTOUFFÉE

1 cup chopped green onion
½ cup butter or margarine
¼ cup chopped fresh parsley
2 pounds crayfish tails, peeled and deveined
1 cup crayfish fat
Salt and pepper to taste
1 teaspoon cornstarch (optional)
Hot cooked rice
Lemon slices

Sauté onion in butter in a large skillet until tender. Stir in parsley, crayfish tails and fat, and salt and pepper; bring to a boil. Reduce heat; simmer, uncovered, 20 minutes.

If a thicker gravy is desired, dissolve cornstarch in a small amount of water, and stir into mixture. Return mixture to a boil. Reduce heat; continue to simmer, uncovered, until desired thickness is reached.

Ladle étouffée over rice in individual serving bowls. Garnish each serving with a lemon slice. Yield: about 1½ quarts.

*Note:* 1 cup butter may be substituted for crayfish fat.

## SHRIMP ÉTOUFFÉE

1 teaspoon salt
½ teaspoon pepper
¼ teaspoon red pepper
3 pounds uncooked medium shrimp, peeled and deveined
1 large onion, chopped
3 stalks celery, cleaned and chopped
½ cup butter or margarine
1 tablespoon cornstarch
½ cup cold water
2 teaspoons tomato paste
3 green onions, chopped
¼ cup chopped fresh parsley
Hot cooked rice

Sprinkle salt and pepper over shrimp; set aside.

Sauté 1 chopped onion and celery in butter in a large skillet until tender.

Dissolve cornstarch in water. Add cornstarch, tomato paste, and shrimp to vegetables; stir well. Cook 10 minutes over low heat, stirring occasionally. Add green onion and parsley; simmer 5 minutes, stirring often.

Spoon over rice in individual serving bowls; serve warm. Yield: about 1 quart.

Culver Pictures

*Shrimp Mull: A gallon of good food with so little effort.*

## SHRIMP MULL

1  cup chopped celery
½  cup diced onion
2  small cloves garlic, minced
3  tablespoons butter or
   margarine
1  quart water
2  (14½-ounce) cans whole
   tomatoes, undrained and
   chopped
1  cup catsup
1  teaspoon Worcestershire
   sauce
¼  teaspoon hot sauce
1  tablespoon salt
1  teaspoon celery seeds
¼  teaspoon pepper
2  pounds uncooked medium
   shrimp, peeled and deveined
1  tablespoon lemon juice
½  cup cracker crumbs
Hot cooked rice

Sauté celery, onion, and garlic
in butter in a small Dutch oven

until tender. Stir in next 8 ingredients; bring to a boil. Reduce heat; cover and simmer 1
hour, stirring occasionally.

Return to a boil; stir in
shrimp and lemon juice. Reduce
heat to medium; cook 5 minutes, stirring constantly. Stir in
cracker crumbs.

Spoon shrimp mixture over
hot cooked rice in individual
serving bowls. Serve immediately. Yield: about 1 gallon.

Give a Southerner, es-
pecially along the
coast, a pound or two
of fresh crustaceans, and he
won't dally too long deciding
which dish to cook. Of
course, he might turn them
into a cold, appetizing cocktail. But there is always rice
in the pantry, and the appe-
tite is ever sharp for one of
those elegant rice combos.
So most likely there will be a
jambalaya, or an étouffée (literally smothered), or even a
mull, any one of which is
prime fare for sharing with a
few very close friends.

# KETTLE COOKERY

## OLD-TIME BEEF STEW

2 pounds lean boneless beef, cut into 1½-inch cubes
2 tablespoons shortening
1 large onion, sliced
1 clove garlic
1 quart hot water
1 tablespoon salt
1 tablespoon lemon juice
1 teaspoon sugar
1 teaspoon Worcestershire sauce
½ teaspoon pepper
½ teaspoon paprika
2 bay leaves
Dash of ground allspice
6 small potatoes, peeled
6 small onions, peeled
3 carrots, cut into 1-inch pieces
¼ cup all-purpose flour
½ cup cold water

Brown beef in hot shortening in a large Dutch oven. Add next 11 ingredients, and bring to a boil. Reduce heat; cover and simmer 1½ hours. Add potatoes, onions, and carrots; cover and simmer an additional hour or until vegetables are tender. Remove and discard bay leaves.

Combine flour and water, stirring to form a smooth paste. Stir into stew; cook over medium heat until thickened and bubbly. Ladle into individual soup bowls, and serve warm. Yield: 2½ quarts.

## CREOLE BEEF STEW

1½ pounds lean beef for stewing, cut into 1-inch cubes
3 potatoes, peeled and cubed
3 ears fresh corn, cut from cob
2 tomatoes, peeled and chopped
2 carrots, scraped and sliced
1 large onion, chopped
1 medium-size green pepper, seeded and chopped
½ pound green beans, snapped and strings removed
1½ teaspoons salt, divided
½ teaspoon pepper
3¼ cups water, divided
1 tablespoon all-purpose flour
¼ teaspoon garlic powder
1½ teaspoons Worcestershire sauce
¼ cup chopped fresh parsley

Arrange meat in bottom of a 3-quart casserole; layer potatoes, corn, tomatoes, carrots, onion, green pepper, and green beans on top of meat. Sprinkle with 1 teaspoon salt and pepper; pour 3 cups water over mixture. Cover and bake at 400° until bubbly; reduce heat to 325°, and continue to bake an additional 2 hours.

Transfer meat and vegetables to a large serving bowl or tureen using a slotted spoon; reserve liquid in casserole. Combine remaining water and flour, stirring to make a paste; add flour mixture, remaining salt, garlic powder, Worcestershire sauce, and parsley to casserole, mixing well. Cook over medium heat, stirring constantly, until gravy thickens.

Spoon gravy over vegetable-meat mixture; serve hot. Yield: about 8 servings.

## BAKED BEEF STEW

½ cup chopped onion
1 clove garlic, minced
¼ cup shortening, divided
2 pounds lean beef for stewing, cut into 1-inch cubes
½ cup all-purpose flour
1 cup tomato juice
2 beef-flavored bouillon cubes
1 (16-ounce) can whole tomatoes, undrained and chopped
1 (8¾-ounce) can whole kernel corn, drained
1 cup diced potatoes
1 cup sliced carrots
½ cup chopped celery
½ cup chili sauce
1¼ teaspoons salt
½ teaspoon freshly ground black pepper

Sauté onion and garlic in 2 tablespoons shortening in a large skillet until tender. Remove onion and garlic with a slotted spoon; set aside. Reserve drippings in skillet.

Dredge meat in flour. Brown meat in reserved pan drippings over medium heat, adding remaining shortening as necessary. Set meat aside.

Bring tomato juice to a boil in a small saucepan; remove from heat, and add bouillon cubes, stirring until dissolved.

Combine onion and garlic, meat, tomato juice mixture, tomatoes, corn, potatoes, carrots, celery, chili sauce, salt, and pepper in an oven-proof 3-quart casserole; stir until well blended. Cover and bake at 325° for 2½ hours, stirring once.

Ladle into individual soup bowls. Serve hot with cornbread. Yield: 3 quarts.

*Old-Time Beef Stew, as it looked suspended over the fire in the old days. Many campers now carry a Dutch oven for simmering stew.*

*Texas ranch hands pose as aproned cook stands among his "batterie de cuisine."*

## TEXAS BEEF STEW

½ cup water
½ cup vinegar
¼ cup catsup
1 tablespoon Worcestershire sauce
1 teaspoon salt
1 teaspoon chili powder
½ teaspoon pepper
1 clove garlic, minced
2 bay leaves
Dash of hot sauce
2 pounds boneless round steak, cut into 1-inch strips
2 large onions, sliced
Hot cooked noodles

Combine water, vinegar, catsup, Worcestershire sauce, salt, chili powder, pepper, garlic, bay leaves, and hot sauce in a small mixing bowl; stir until well combined. Place meat in a small Dutch oven, and pour vinegar mixture evenly over top. Cover and refrigerate 1 hour, turning meat once.

Place onions on top of meat mixture; cover and simmer 1½ hours or until meat is tender. Remove and discard bay leaves. Serve stew immediately over hot cooked noodles. Yield: 4 to 6 servings.

## WINE BEEF STEW WITH DUMPLINGS

2 cups Burgundy or other dry red wine
2 cups water
1 tablespoon beef flavor base
2 teaspoons beau monde seasoning
½ teaspoon dried whole thyme, crushed
¼ teaspoon dried whole rosemary, crushed
¼ teaspoon garlic powder
2 pounds lean beef for stewing, cut into 1-inch cubes
2 tablespoons butter or margarine
4 medium onions, peeled and quartered
2 cups sliced carrots
Dumplings (recipe follows)

Combine first 7 ingredients in a large mixing bowl; let stand 10 minutes.

Brown beef on all sides in butter in a large Dutch oven. Add wine mixture to beef; bring to a boil. Reduce heat; cover and simmer 1 hour. Add onion and carrots; cover and simmer 30 minutes or until vegetables are tender.

Prepare dumplings. Drop batter by tablespoonfuls into simmering meat mixture, allowing room for dumplings to expand during cooking process. Cook, uncovered, 10 minutes. Cover and cook an additional 10 minutes.

Spoon into individual serving bowls, and serve immediately. Yield: 6 to 8 servings.

Dumplings:

2 cups buttermilk biscuit mix
½ teaspoon beau monde seasoning
¼ teaspoon dried whole rosemary, crushed
¾ cup milk

Combine first 3 ingredients in a small mixing bowl. Add milk; stir just until dry ingredients are moistened. Yield: batter for 14 dumplings.

# CARBONADES À LA FLAMANDE

2 pounds lean beef for stewing, cut into ½-inch cubes
¼ cup all-purpose flour
¼ cup vegetable oil
1 large onion, sliced
3 cloves garlic, minced
¼ cup chopped fresh parsley
2 tablespoons red wine vinegar, divided
1½ tablespoons firmly packed dark brown sugar
1 tablespoon dried whole thyme
1 teaspoon salt
½ teaspoon pepper
1 bay leaf
1 (10½-ounce) can beef consommé, undiluted
1 (12-ounce) can beer
Hot buttered noodles

Dredge meat in flour; sauté in hot oil in a large skillet until browned. Transfer meat to an oven-proof 3-quart casserole, reserving drippings in skillet.

Sauté onion and garlic in pan drippings until tender; remove with a slotted spoon and add to meat. Discard pan drippings. Add parsley, 1 tablespoon vinegar, brown sugar, thyme, salt, pepper, and bay leaf to meat mixture, stirring well.

Add beef consommé to skillet. Bring consommé to a boil, scraping any browned bits from skillet. Pour consommé and beer over meat mixture, stirring until well blended. Cover and bake at 325° for 2 hours; remove from oven, and stir in remaining vinegar. Bring to a boil over medium heat, stirring frequently. Remove from heat; remove and discard bay leaf.

Serve stew immediately over hot buttered noodles. Yield: 6 servings.

*Meatball Stew offers one of the best ways to use ground beef. An easy whole meal when loaded with flavorful and nutritious vegetables.*

# MEATBALL STEW

1½ pounds ground chuck
¾ cup soft breadcrumbs
1 tablespoon dried minced onion
1¾ teaspoons salt, divided
½ teaspoon pepper
¼ cup vegetable oil
3½ cups water
1 (6-ounce) can tomato paste
½ teaspoon dried whole thyme
1 clove garlic, minced
1 bay leaf
1 cup cubed potato
1 cup sliced celery
1 cup sliced carrots
2 medium onions, chopped
¼ cup chopped fresh parsley

Combine ground chuck, breadcrumbs, minced onion, ¾ teaspoon salt, and pepper, mixing well. Shape mixture into 1½-inch meatballs; brown in oil in a large skillet over medium heat. Drain off drippings.

Combine meatballs, water, tomato paste, remaining salt, thyme, garlic, and bay leaf; cover and simmer 30 minutes.

Stir in remaining ingredients; cover and simmer 30 minutes, stirring occasionally. Remove and discard bay leaf.

Serve stew immediately in individual soup bowls. Yield: 2 quarts.

*Ad for the McCormick reaper romanticizes the machine that helped transform the wilderness into farmland.*

## PIONEER CORN STEW

1 pound lean ground beef
1 medium onion, chopped
½ cup chopped green pepper
1 (17-ounce) can whole kernel corn, undrained
1 (10¾-ounce) can tomato soup, undiluted
2 teaspoons sugar
1 teaspoon salt

Sauté meat, onion, and green pepper in a large saucepan until meat is browned and vegetables are tender. Stir in remaining ingredients, mixing well. Bring to a boil. Reduce heat; simmer, uncovered, 20 minutes. Serve in individual soup bowls. Yield: 1½ quarts.

## VEAL STEW

2 pounds boneless veal, cut into 1½-inch cubes
1 teaspoon salt
½ teaspoon pepper
¼ cup all-purpose flour
2 tablespoons vegetable oil
1 quart water
2 cups sliced, peeled potatoes
½ cup sliced carrots
¼ cup chopped turnips
1 small onion, thinly sliced

Sprinkle veal with salt and pepper; dredge in flour. Heat oil in a large Dutch oven; brown veal on all sides. Add water; bring to a boil. Reduce heat; cover and simmer 1½ hours. Stir in remaining ingredients; cover and simmer 30 minutes or until vegetables are tender.

Ladle stew into individual serving bowls, and serve hot. Yield: 1½ quarts.

## HUNGARIAN GOULASH

½ cup all-purpose flour
1 tablespoon paprika
1½ teaspoons salt
2 pounds boneless veal cutlets, cut into 1-inch cubes
3 tablespoons bacon drippings
1 small onion, finely chopped
1 clove garlic, chopped
1 cup hot water
Hot cooked noodles
Fresh parsley sprigs

Combine flour, paprika, and salt in a large bowl; mix well. Dredge veal in flour; coat well. Brown veal in drippings in a large skillet. Add onion, garlic, and water. Cover; simmer 45 minutes or until veal is tender.

Serve over noodles; garnish with parsley. Yield: 6 servings.

## CAESAR STEW

2 pounds boneless lamb
  shoulder
1½ cups hot water
3 tablespoons dried minced
  onion
1 bay leaf
2 pounds fresh spinach,
  cleaned and chopped
3 cups diced, peeled tomato
1½ teaspoons salt
1 teaspoon dried rosemary
  leaves, crushed
½ teaspoon pepper

Trim excess fat from meat, and set fat aside. Cut meat into 1-inch cubes; set aside.

Cook reserved fat in a large Dutch oven over medium heat; remove and discard fat, reserving drippings in Dutch oven. Add meat to Dutch oven; brown on all sides. Stir in water, onion, and bay leaf; bring to a boil. Reduce heat; cover and simmer 1 hour.

Add remaining ingredients; bring to a boil. Reduce heat; cover and simmer 10 minutes or until spinach is tender, stirring occasionally. Remove and discard bay leaf.

Ladle into serving bowls, and serve immediately. Yield: 1½ quarts.

There are some clues in the names of recipes that trigger a sense of familiarity. Irish Stew may reasonably be expected to be made of lamb, not browned; we know we are about to make a white stew. Scottish "Brew" (page 132), in a collection of stews, will likewise be a lamb stew, as we know all British Islanders were mutton eaters, and we may expect barley. Hungarian Goulash? We look for paprika. But some recipe names are pure whimsy. The pioneers, after all, had no canned soup!

## IRISH STEW

2 pounds boneless lamb
  shoulder, cut into 2-inch
  cubes
1 quart water
¼ cup chopped fresh celery
  leaves
2 sprigs fresh parsley
1 bay leaf
2 teaspoons salt
3 medium potatoes, peeled
  and quartered
2 cups cubed rutabaga
2 small onions, chopped
3 tablespoons water
2 tablespoons all-purpose
  flour
1 tablespoon Worcestershire
  sauce

Combine meat, 1 quart water, celery leaves, parsley, bay leaf, and salt in a medium Dutch oven. Cover and simmer 1½ hours. Stir in potatoes, rutabaga, and onion; cover and simmer an additional 45 minutes or until vegetables are tender.

Combine 3 tablespoons water, flour, and Worcestershire sauce; stir until smooth. Stir flour mixture into stew, and cook over medium heat until slightly thickened. Remove and discard bay leaf.

Serve stew hot in individual bowls. Yield: about 2½ quarts.

*Irish Stew (front) and Caesar Stew: hearty fare indeed.*

*1890 engraving of a sheepherder and his herd.*

Collection of Kit Barry, Brattleboro, Vermont

## SCOTTISH BREW

4 whole cloves
1 medium onion
1 (3-pound) leg of lamb roast, cooked
2 quarts water
2 teaspoons salt
¼ teaspoon freshly ground black pepper
1 bay leaf
3 carrots, scraped and sliced
2 small turnips, peeled and sliced
2 stalks celery, diced
¼ cup uncooked pearl barley
¼ cup Scotch whiskey
½ teaspoon dried whole marjoram

Insert whole cloves in onion. Combine onion, roast, water, salt, pepper, and bay leaf in a large Dutch oven; bring to a boil. Reduce heat; cover and simmer 1½ hours.

Remove roast from stew; cool slightly. Remove meat from bone, discarding bone. Chop meat into bite-size pieces, and return to stew; cool to room temperature. Refrigerate stew until all fat has risen to the top; skim off and discard fat. Remove whole onion from stew; re-move and discard cloves. Chop onion, and return to stew.

Add remaining ingredients to stew, stirring until well blended; bring to a boil. Reduce heat; cover and simmer 45 minutes. Uncover and cook an additional 30 minutes. Remove and discard bay leaf.

Serve stew immediately in individual serving bowls. Yield: 3 quarts.

## CHICKEN STEW

1 (5-pound) stewing hen, cut up
3 quarts water
1 medium onion, quartered
1 tablespoon salt
1 teaspoon pepper
½ teaspoon dried whole oregano
½ teaspoon rubbed sage
1 (17-ounce) can whole kernel corn, drained
3 cups diced potato
6 stalks celery, sliced
6 medium carrots, scraped and sliced
¼ cup all-purpose flour
⅓ cup water

Combine chicken, water, onion, salt, pepper, oregano, and sage in a large Dutch oven; bring to a boil. Reduce heat; cover and simmer 2½ hours or until chicken is tender. Remove chicken from broth; cool. Bone chicken, and cut meat into bite-size pieces; discard bones, and set meat aside.

Add chicken, corn, potatoes, celery, and carrots to broth; simmer, uncovered, 1½ hours or until vegetables are tender.

Combine flour and water, stirring until smooth. Add flour mixture to stew; cook, stirring frequently, until stew is thickened. Serve immediately in individual bowls. Yield: 2½ quarts.

# BOUCHÉES À LA REINE

1 (6-pound) stewing hen
1 large onion, quartered
1 stalk celery, halved
3 quarts water
¾ pound fresh mushrooms, sliced
1 large onion, chopped
¼ cup butter or margarine
¼ cup all-purpose flour
¼ cup chopped pimiento
2 teaspoons salt
½ teaspoon pepper
8 Kaiser rolls

Combine first 4 ingredients in a large Dutch oven; bring to a boil. Reduce heat; cover and simmer 2 hours. Remove chicken from broth; let cool slightly. Remove meat from bones, discarding bones; chop meat into bite-size pieces. Strain broth, reserving 1 quart. Discard quartered onion and celery. Reserve remaining broth for use in other recipes.

Sauté mushrooms and chopped onion in butter in a large Dutch oven until tender. Stir in flour. Cook over medium heat 5 minutes, stirring constantly. Gradually add reserved 1 quart chicken broth; cook over medium heat, stirring constantly, until thickened and bubbly. Stir in reserved chicken, pimiento, salt, and pepper. Remove from heat, and keep warm.

Cut a slice from top of each Kaiser roll to form a lid; set aside. Remove soft center from each roll, and reserve for other uses, leaving shells intact. Place rolls and lids on baking sheets. Bake at 350° for 8 minutes or until lightly browned and crisp.

Spoon warm chicken mixture into rolls. Place each filled roll and lid on an individual serving plate, and serve immediately. Yield: 8 servings.

## OLD SOUTH STEW

1 (3½-pound) broiler-fryer, cut up
1 (1-pound) meaty soup bone
2 quarts water
1 tablespoon plus 1½ teaspoons salt
½ teaspoon pepper
1 hot red pepper pod
2 medium onions, chopped
1 (16-ounce) package frozen butter beans
1 (16-ounce) package frozen cut okra
2½ pounds ripe tomatoes, peeled and chopped
12 ears fresh yellow corn, cut from cob
2 tablespoons Worcestershire sauce
1 teaspoon sugar

Combine first 6 ingredients in a large stockpot. Bring to a boil. Reduce heat; cover and simmer 1½ hours. Remove chicken and soup bone from broth; cool slightly. Remove meat from bones; chop meat into bite-size pieces. Discard bones and red pepper pod.

Return meat to broth. Stir in remaining ingredients. Bring to a boil. Reduce heat; cover and simmer 30 minutes. Uncover and simmer an additional 30 minutes.

Ladle stew into individual soup bowls. Serve hot with cornbread, if desired. Yield: about 1½ gallons.

*Bouchées à la Reine: Crunchy toasted Kaiser rolls contain chicken and mushroom filling. Luncheon, anyone?*

133

## CAMP STEW

*Texas ranch hands pose with piping hot stew as aproned cook stands among his "batterie de cuisine."*

2 pounds meaty soup bones
½ pound lean pork, cut into 1-inch cubes
½ pound veal, cut into 1-inch cubes
½ pound lean beef for stewing, cut into 1-inch cubes
2 bay leaves
2 teaspoons salt
½ teaspoon pepper
¼ teaspoon red pepper
1 gallon water
3 large potatoes, peeled and cubed
2 green peppers, seeded and chopped
1 large onion, chopped
1 stalk celery, cleaned and chopped
2 (17-ounce) cans whole kernel corn, drained
2 (16-ounce) cans whole tomatoes, undrained
¼ cup plus 1 tablespoon catsup
2 tablespoons Worcestershire sauce
¼ pound calves' liver, cut into small pieces

Combine soup bones, pork, veal, beef, bay leaves, salt, pepper, and water in a large stockpot; bring to a boil. Reduce heat; cover and simmer 3 hours. Remove from heat, and cool to room temperature.

Remove soup bones from broth; remove meat from bones, discarding bones. Coarsely chop meat, and return to broth. Cover and refrigerate overnight.

Skim off and discard fat from surface of broth. Add potatoes, green pepper, onion, celery, corn, tomatoes, catsup, and Worcestershire sauce; bring to a boil. Reduce heat; cover and simmer 30 minutes. Add liver; cover and simmer an additional 30 minutes. Remove and discard bay leaves.

Ladle stew into individual serving bowls; serve hot. Yield: about 5 quarts.

Texas has its barbecues, the Eastern Shore its oyster roasts, and the Gulf Shore its shrimp boils. Many a political candidacy has been sprung on a population rallied 'round a sandy podium. Inland, there are stews: not only the good meaty mainstays of places like the Cataloochie Ranch and Felder's Campground in Mississippi, but also Brunswick Stew and Burgoo. In Kentucky, anyone within sight of those huge burgoo vats is usually also within earshot of a practicing politician. By the time the oratory begins, the voter is sated, ready to listen.

## BRUNSWICK STEW

1 (5-pound) stewing hen
1 (3-pound) chuck roast, cooked, cooled, and shredded
1 (3-pound) pork loin roast, cooked, cooled, and shredded
5 cups beef broth
3 (16-ounce) cans whole tomatoes, undrained and chopped
2 (12-ounce) cans whole kernel corn
1 (15-ounce) can tomato sauce
3 large onions, chopped
1½ cups catsup
½ cup vinegar
⅓ cup Worcestershire sauce
1 tablespoon salt
2 teaspoons pepper
2 teaspoons hot sauce
1 teaspoon garlic salt
1 teaspoon lemon juice

Place chicken in a large Dutch oven; add water to cover. Bring to a boil; cover and simmer 2 hours or until chicken is tender. Remove chicken from broth; cool. Bone chicken, and grind meat using coarse blade of meat grinder.

Transfer 5 cups chicken broth to a large stockpot; reserve remaining broth for use in other recipes. Add ground chicken and remaining ingredients, stirring until well blended. Bring to a boil. Reduce heat; simmer, uncovered, 3 hours.

Ladle stew into individual bowls, and serve hot. Yield: about 1½ gallons.

## BURGOO

1 (5-pound) stewing hen
2 pounds pork shank
2 pounds veal shank
2 pounds beef shank
2 pounds breast of lamb
2 gallons water
3 large potatoes, peeled and diced
3 large onions, chopped
3 large carrots, scraped and thinly sliced
2 green peppers, seeded and chopped
2 cups shredded cabbage
1 (28-ounce) can whole tomatoes, undrained
1 (17-ounce) can whole kernel corn, drained
1 cup lima beans
1 bunch fresh parsley, chopped
2 hot red pepper pods
1 tablespoon salt
½ teaspoon red pepper
1 tablespoon plus 1 teaspoon Worcestershire sauce

Combine chicken, pork, veal, beef, lamb, and water in a large stockpot; bring to a boil. Reduce heat; cover and simmer 2 hours or until meat is tender.

Remove meat from broth; cool slightly. Remove meat from bones, discarding bones. Coarsely chop meat, and set aside.

Skim off and discard fat from surface of broth. Combine broth, meat, and remaining ingredients in stockpot. Bring to a boil. Reduce heat; simmer, uncovered, 4½ hours or until thickened, stirring occasionally. Discard pepper pods.

Ladle stew into individual serving bowls; serve hot. Yield: about 2 gallons.

## KENTUCKY MULLIGAN STEW

1 (5-pound) stewing hen, cut up
1 tablespoon salt
½ teaspoon pepper
1 gallon plus 1 pint water, divided
1 large onion, sliced
½ cup vegetable oil
2½ pounds lean beef for stewing, cut into 1-inch cubes
1 pound veal, cut into 1-inch cubes
½ cup all-purpose flour
4 (16-ounce) cans whole tomatoes, undrained
3 (12-ounce) cans whole kernel corn, drained
2 (8½-ounce) cans lima beans, drained
3 cups frozen green peas
½ teaspoon garlic powder
½ teaspoon paprika
¼ teaspoon angostura bitters

Combine chicken, salt, pepper, and 2 quarts water in a large stockpot; bring to a boil. Reduce heat; simmer, uncovered, 1½ hours or until chicken is tender.

Remove chicken from broth; cool slightly. Remove meat from bones, discarding bones. Coarsely chop meat; set aside. Set broth aside in stockpot.

Sauté onion in oil in a large skillet until tender. Remove onion with a slotted spoon, and drain well, reserving oil in skillet. Set onion aside.

Dredge beef and veal in flour; brown meat in reserved oil. Drain well.

Add reserved chicken, sautéed onion, and browned meat to broth; add 2 quarts water. Bring to a boil. Reduce heat; simmer, uncovered, 4 hours, stirring occasionally.

Stir in tomatoes, corn, lima beans, peas, garlic powder, paprika, angostura bitters, and remaining water; continue to simmer, uncovered, 1 hour, stirring occasionally.

Ladle stew into individual serving bowls; serve warm. Yield: about 2¼ gallons.

## CRAYFISH STEW

1 pound steamed crayfish tails, peeled, deveined, and chopped
1½ cups seasoned, dry breadcrumbs
1 medium onion, finely chopped and divided
¼ cup chopped green onion
2 stalks celery, finely chopped
2 small cloves garlic, minced and divided
1 teaspoon salt, divided
½ teaspoon pepper, divided
¼ teaspoon red pepper, divided
4 eggs, beaten
1 quart water, divided
2 tablespoons butter or margarine
2 tablespoons all-purpose flour
1 (6-ounce) can tomato paste
2 teaspoons sugar
½ cup vegetable oil
Hot cooked rice

Combine crayfish, breadcrumbs, half of chopped onion, green onion, celery, 1 clove minced garlic, ½ teaspoon salt, ¼ teaspoon pepper, and ⅛ teaspoon red pepper in a large mixing bowl; stir until well blended. Add eggs and ¼ cup plus 2 tablespoons water; mix well.

Shape mixture into 1½-inch balls. Place on a waxed paper-lined baking sheet; cover and chill 1 hour.

Melt butter in a large Dutch oven over low heat. Add flour; stir until blended. Cook, stirring constantly, until roux is the color of a copper penny. Add remaining onion and garlic; cook until tender.

Add tomato paste, sugar, and remaining water, salt, and pepper; cook over medium-low heat, stirring until thickened. Remove from heat; set aside.

Brown crayfish balls in hot oil in a large skillet over medium heat. Drain on paper towels.

Add crayfish balls to roux in Dutch oven; bring to a boil. Reduce heat; cover and simmer 1½ hours. Serve over hot cooked rice in warm soup bowls. Yield: 8 to 10 servings.

## BOUILLABAISSE

1 red snapper head
1 medium onion, sliced
½ cup chopped fresh parsley
4 sprigs fresh thyme, chopped
1½ quarts water
1¼ cups Chablis or other dry white wine
1 (14½-ounce) can whole tomatoes, drained and chopped
Juice of half a lemon
1 teaspoon salt, divided
½ teaspoon pepper, divided
⅛ teaspoon red pepper
3 sprigs fresh parsley, minced
3 sprigs fresh thyme, minced
3 cloves garlic, minced
3 bay leaves, crumbled
¼ teaspoon ground allspice
¾ pound redfish fillets
¾ pound red snapper fillets
1½ cups finely chopped onion
2 tablespoons olive oil
Toast points
Lemon slices
Fresh parsley sprigs

Combine first 5 ingredients in a small Dutch oven; bring to a boil. Reduce heat; simmer, uncovered, until mixture is reduced to 1 pint. Strain mixture through several layers of damp cheesecloth, discarding fish head, vegetables, and spices. Set fish stock aside.

Combine wine, tomatoes, lemon juice, fish stock, ½ teaspoon salt, ¼ teaspoon pepper, and red pepper in skillet. Cook over medium heat 25 minutes or until mixture is reduced by half. Set aside; keep warm.

Combine minced parsley, thyme, garlic, bay leaves, remaining salt and pepper, and allspice in a small bowl; blend well. Rub herb mixture over surface of fillets; set aside.

Sauté chopped onion in olive oil in a large skillet until tender; set onion aside, reserving oil in skillet. Add fillets to skillet; top with onion. Cover; cook over medium heat 10 minutes.

Transfer fillets to a serving platter lined with toast points. Pour reserved sauce over fish, and garnish with lemon slices and fresh parsley sprigs. Serve immediately. Yield: 4 servings.

## PINE BARK STEW

½ pound sliced bacon
2 large onions, chopped
2 quarts water
6 large potatoes, peeled and diced
2 (14½-ounce) cans whole tomatoes, undrained and chopped
2 pounds catfish fillets, cut into bite-size pieces
1 cup catsup
Salt and pepper to taste

Cook bacon in a large stockpot until crisp; drain bacon on paper towels, reserving ¼ cup drippings in stockpot. Crumble bacon, and set aside.

Sauté onion in drippings until tender. Stir in water, potatoes, tomatoes, and reserved bacon; bring to a boil. Reduce heat; cover and simmer 3 hours. Stir in catfish; cover and continue to simmer an additional 30 minutes. Stir in catsup and salt and pepper; cook until thoroughly heated.

Ladle stew into individual serving bowls. Serve hot. Yield: 1½ gallons.

*Mother and daughter cook together. 1915 photo typifies the way skills were handed down in the South.*

# ACKNOWLEDGMENTS

Avgolemono Soup, Beaufort Cream of Crab Soup, Cream of Carrot Soup, Huguenot Onion Soup, Jefferson Davis' Oyster Soup, Savannah Okra Soup, Scottish Brew adapted from *Savannah Sampler Cookbook* by Margaret Wayt DeBolt, ©1978. By permission of The Donning/Company Publishers, Norfolk, Virginia.

Barley Broth, French Broth adapted from *Martha Washington Cookbook* by the Virginia Historical Society, Richmond, Virginia.

Bean and Bacon Chowder, Cream of Wild Rice Soup, Driskill Hotel Cheese Soup, Frijole-Cheese Soup adapted from *Cartwright Cuisine, Recipes from Eight Generations of a Texas Family,* compiled by Marilyn Mays Bloemendal, Patty Cartwright Harvey, and Mollie Lupe Lasater. Published in 1983. By permission of the Cartwright Family, Ft. Worth, Texas.

Beef Soup with Liver Dumplings, Chicken Noodle Soup, Sauerkraut Soup adapted from *Generation to Generation,* compiled by Barbara Dybala and Helen Macik, ©1980. By permission of the Historical Society of the Czech Club, Dallas, Texas.

Brunswick Stew courtesy of Marty Becknell, Oxford, Alabama.

Cajun Gumbo, Easy Hearty Chili, Red Bean Soup from Avery Island adapted from *Helen Exum's Cookbook,* ©1982. By permission of Helen McDonald Exum, Chattanooga, Tennessee.

Carbonades à la Flamande, Cream of Shrimp Soup, Crayfish Stew, Duck Gumbo, Green Onion Soup, Baked-in-a-Pumpkin Soup, Shrimp and Oyster Jambalaya, Turkey-Sausage Gumbo adapted from *La Bonne Cuisine.* Published in 1980 by La Bonne Cuisine, River Ridge, Louisiana.

Charles Bronger's Louisville Turtle Soup, Ham Bone Soup, Rice Balls adapted from *Out of Kentucky Kitchens* by Marion Flexner, ©1949. By permission of Franklin Watts, Inc., New York.

Charleston White Bisque, Clam Bisque, Seafood Gumbo, Seasoned Soup Stock adapted from *Charleston Receipts* by The Junior League of Charleston, ©1950. By permission of The Junior League of Charleston, South Carolina.

Chicken Gumbo Filé, Cream of Cucumber Soup, Old-Time Beef Stew, Pioneer Corn Stew, Quick Tomato Soup, Senate Restaurant Bean Soup, Spinach Soup adapted from *The Nashville Cookbook* by Nashville Area Home Economics Association, ©1977. By permission of Nashville Area Home Economics Association, Tennessee.

Chicken Mulligatawny adapted from *Dear Daugher* by Eula Mae Tucker. By permission of Eula Mae Tucker, Marionville, Missouri.

Chicken Soup and Filled Dumplings adapted from *Good Cooks Never Lack Friends* by Sisterhood Agudath Achim Synagogue, ©1978. By permission of Sisterhood Agudath Achim, Savannah, Georgia.

Chicken Stew courtesy of Marge Steen, Chesapeake, Virginia.

Chilled Raspberry Soup, Cold Peach Soup, Scandinavian Fruit Soup adapted from *Gallery Buffet Soup Cookbook* by Dallas Museum of Fine Arts League, ©1977. By permission of Dallas Museum of Fine Arts, Texas.

Cold Curried Squash Soup adapted from *Georgia Heritage - Treasured Recipes.* Pulished in 1979 by The National Society of the Colonial Dames of America in the State of Georgia.

Cold Cherry Soup adapted from *Guten Appetit!,* compiled by the Sophienburg Museum, ©1978. By permission of Sophienburg Museum, New Braunfels, Texas.

Cold Weather Chili adapted from *The Mississippi Cookbook,* compiled by the Home Economics Division of the Mississippi Cooperative Extension Service. By permission of University Press of Mississippi, Jackson.

Collard Green Soup from Las Novedades Restaurant, Florida Fish Chowder by Mrs. David J. Kadyk, Tomato Bouillon by Mrs Brightman J. Skinner, Jr. adapted from *The Gasparilla Cookbook* by The Junior League of Tampa, ©1961. By permission of The Junior League of Tampa, Florida.

Crab Gumbo adapted from *Chesapeake Bay Crab Recipes,* published in Annapolis, Maryland.

Crayfish Étouffée adapted from Louisiana Legacy by the Thibodaux Service League, Thibodaux, Louisiana.

Cream of Chestnut Soup, Lettuce Soup, Royal Custard adapted from *Southern Cooking* by Mrs. S.R Dull, ©1941 by S.R. Dull. By permission of Grosset and Dunlap, New York.

Cream of Eggplant Soup adapted from *Gulf Gourmet* by Westminster Academy Mothers Club, ©1979. By permission of Westminster Academy, Gulfport, Mississippi.

Cream of Zucchini Soup, Indian River Soup, Watercress Soup adapted from *Palm Beach Entertains - Then and Now* by The Junior League of the Palm Beaches, Inc., ©1976. By permission of The Junior League of the Beaches, Inc., Florida.

Creamy Herb Potato Soup adapted from *Old Shaker Recipes*, ©1982. By permission of Bear Wallow Books, Nashville, Indiana.

Egg Soup adapted from *Two Hundred Years of Charleston Cooking*, edited by Lettie Gay, ©1976. By permission of the University of South Carolina Press.

Filled Noodle Soup courtesy of Dr. Jackie Nixon-Fulton, Lancaster, Texas.

Golden Chicken Soup, Homemade Noodles, Lentil Soup, Meaty Chili adapted from *Keneseth Israel Sisterhood Cookbook* by Keneseth Israel Sisterhood, ©1971. By permission of Keneseth Israel Sisterhood, Louisville, Kentucky.

Home-Style Tomato Soup, Kentucky Mulligan Stew, Oxtail Vegetable Soup adapted from *Famous Kentucky Recipes*, compiled by Cabbage Patch Circle, Louisville, Kentucky.

Illustration on back cover courtesy of Staples & Charles.

Lima Bean Chowder, Southern Jugged Soup adapted from *The United States Regional Cook Book*, edited by Ruth Berolzheimer, ©1941. By permission of Consolidated Book Pulishers, Chicago.

Lola's Gazpacho courtesy of Lola Ceballos, Birmingham, Alabama.

Louisiana Gumbo adapted from *The Monticello Cookbook* by The University of Virginia Hospital Circle, ©1950. By permission of the Dietz Press, Richmond, Virginia.

Manhattan-Style Clam Chowder, Statehouse Oyster Chowder adapted from *Maryland Seafood Cookbook III* by The Maryland Department of Economic and Community Development, Annapolis, Maryland.

Matzo Balls, Minestrone adapted from *Revel* by The Junior League of Shreveport, Inc., ©1980. By permission of Books Unlimited, Shreveport, Louisiana.

Mexican Meatball Soup adapted from *Seasoned with Sun* by the Junior League of El Paso, Texas, ©1974. By permission of the Junior Leage of El Paso, Inc., Texas.

Mushroom and Barley Chowder, Sweet and Sour Cabbage Soup adapted from *To Serve with Love* by the Women's Auxiliary of Wheeling Hospital, Wheeling, West Virginia.

New England Clam Chowder adapted from *Winston-Salem's Heritage of Hospitality* by the Junior League of Winston-Salem, ©1975. By permission of the Junior League of Winston-Salem, North Carolina.

Oyster Creole adapted from *Maryland Seafood Cookbook I* by The Maryland Department of Economic and Community Development, Annapolis, Maryland.

Parmesan Breadsticks courtesy of *Creative Ideas for Living* magazine, April, 1985 issue.

Parmesan Rosettes, Sesame Crisps, Wheat Crackers adapted from *Holiday Gifts from a Country Kitchen* by Mary Reynolds Smith. Published by Potpourri Press, Greensboro, North Carolina.

Potato Soup adapted from *Maryland's Way* by Mrs. Lewis R. Andrews and Mrs. J. Reaney Kelly. By permission of The Hammond-Harwood House Association, Annapolis, Maryland.

Prize-Winning Spicy Chili, Spinach and Crabmeat Soup adapted from *Delicioso!* by The Junior League of Corpus Christi, ©1982. By permission of The Junior League of Corpus Christi, Texas.

Salsify Bisque adapted from *Welcome Back to Pleasant Hill* by Elizabeth C. Kremer, ©1977. By permission of Shakertown at Pleasant Hill, Harrodsburg, Kentucky.

Seafood-Mushroom Soup courtesy of Chalet Suzanne, Lake Wales, Florida.

Spaetzle adapted from *Fredericksburg Home Kitchen Cookbook*, published by The Fredericksburg Home Kitchen Cookbook Central Committee, 1957. By permission of The Fredericksburg Home Kitchen Cookbook Central Committee, Fredericksburg, Texas.

Strawberry Soup, Summer Vegetable Soup adapted from *Pass the Plate* by Episcopal Churchwomen and Friends of Christ Episcopal Church, New Bern, North Carolina.

Texas Beef Stew courtesy of Gebhardt's Chili Powder Company, San Antonio, Texas.

Tomato-Vermicelli Soup adapted from *Come Cook With Us: A Treasury of Greek Cooking* by The Hellenic Woman's Club, ©1967. By permission of The Hellenic Woman's Club, Norfolk, Virginia.

Tortilla Soup courtesy of Ann Wallace, McAllen, Texas.

Venison Chili courtesy of Mrs. Clint Wyrick, Garland, Texas.

# INDEX